First Printing Lock 'n Load Publishing
Copyright © 2019 Lock 'n Load Publis.
All Rights Reserved.
Printed in the United States of America in the State of Colorado
Lock 'n Load Publishing LLC
1027 North Market Plaza, Suite 107 - 146
Pueblo West, Colorado, 81007
Rev 11
ISBN: 978-17-331-0411-1

M000163654

CONTENTS

INTRODUCTION

Welcome to the second edition of "Storm and Steel" which we updated the title to Storm and Steel Second Wave. When David Heath asked me to write this new edition of the book, I wasn't sure what I would add or change. The original seemed to be enjoyed by many people so why mess with it? Upon re-reading the book, I soon realized there were many reasons to update the story.

The first thing I wanted to do was make some alterations to the tone. My original intention was for the second act to feel similar to "Apocalypse Now" or "Heart of Darkness" as Mohr travels through a hellish landscape that takes him deeper and deeper into a nightmarish ordeal. I had overwritten some of the scenes where it would have been better to leave things to the reader's imagination. Sometimes, less is more. In other cases, I expanded on things that weren't clear or were confusing.

The writing is much smoother in this new edition with an emphasis on "show don't tell". Descriptions of character actions are inferred rather than spelled out directly in most places now. Hopefully, this lends the action a greater sense of immediacy and a "you are there" feeling to the battles. Some changes to the writing are the equivalent of a plastic surgeon's nip or tuck. Others were more drastic.

After finishing the original book I regretted not building up the tension between Captain Mohr and Lieutenant Schmitt. Despite spelling out the source of their animosity in the book's early chapters, the confrontation at Platlling felt rushed. To that end, I added a prologue that goes deeper into the problems of 2nd

Company and more fully explains Mohr's impossible task and the opposition he faces.

For those who are interested in the hardware, I've included a fictional magazine article about the Leopard 1 that is written long after the war. It describes the basic advantages and drawbacks of the MBT and how it performed in the war. This helps shed further light on why Mohr chooses certain tactics and expands on the dangers he faces while fighting in an aging tank.

The production values for the book have increased exponentially. As a self-published author, I had little money to spend on illustrations and book covers for the first edition. I had to turn to Photoshop tutorials to learn how to make maps. Against my better judgement, the awful but functional map of Grafling made it into the first edition of the book. This time around, the reader benefits from a professional illustrator and a company that gives the reader a quality product from top to bottom.

I should add that this book moves the action to Keith Tracton's "World at War 85" setting and I have adapted certain aspects of the story in order to agree with his the canon of his universe. Keith was kind enough to offer advice on various aspects of the story and for that I am grateful. I am also humbled that he took several scenes from this book and adapted them for an expansion to the game series. Thank you, Keith.

I'd also like to say a huge thanks to David Heath, the owner of Lock 'n Load Publishing, who saw the potential in my books and myself and took a chance. The patience and guidance he has shown throughout this process has been immeasurable.

Brad Smith

DEDICATION

For Maya and Hiro.

ACKNOWLEDGMENTS

Once again, I find myself in debt to Keith Tracton and David Heath. It was Keith who read and enjoyed "Storm and Steel" then recommended it to David, who then got in touch with me. One e-mail led to another and the rest, as they say, is history. I want to give Keith another huge thanks for using that golden voice of his to breathe life into the audiobook.

As always, I owe thanks to my family. My wife, Maya, put up with the stress of living with a writer whose mood shifted as he steered an unsteady course over each successive chapter until the book was finally ready to be published. My son Hiro was there to remind me to take a break once in a while and be a dad. Thanks buddy!

My inspiration for book came from many places but many were modeled with the help of Jim Day's "MBT" expansion "FRG". Though the Czechoslovakians weren't available, I used comparable Russian equipment to fill out their order of battle. The flow of the first battle in this book owes as much to Scenario 13 as it does to my own imagination.

I would like to thank the wargaming community as a whole, which showed an incredible amount of enthusiasm for my books and games. I am humbled by your support and I hope you enjoy this story.

STORM AND STEEL

SECOND WAVE

A WORLD AT WAR 85 NOVEL

BRAD SMITH

PROLOGUE

April 1, 1985
Grafenwöhr Training Area, West Germany
"You're all dead!"

The American judge stood in the road and waved a palm across the breadth of Captain Kurt Mohr's three tank platoons. After announcing their gloomy fate, he glanced down at his watch and declared a break for lunch.

The morning's training exercise was over and the West Germans had suffered yet another loss – the third in three days. Mohr shook his head and jumped down from his Leopard 1 into the high wet grass.

Behind his vehicle sat the hulking angular outlines of four M1s of the 2nd Armored Cavalry Regiment. Somehow, the Americans had plowed straight through Mohr's rear and snuck up behind the main body of his company. Another minute more and Lieutenant Kessel's platoon would have finally taken up an ambush position while Unger and Meier's men provided overwatch on the valley below.

How on earth had that happened?

Lieutenant Schmitt had been ordered to guard against such a possibility by taking on the role of rear security. Mohr had told him to deploy his tanks on the ridgeline to the north. The long strip of high grass provided an excellent view of the only possible enemy approaches to their position. Despite that, the Americans had found their way through the perimeter without a scratch and "killed" everybody. It was hard for Mohr to shake the feeling that he had been sabotaged.

The Abrams platoon wheeled right in a tight column formation and drove off east, no doubt headed for the giant mess hall near Tower Barracks. Their squadron commander would surely be waiting for them, ready to heap on the hearty praise that came with beating the West Germans on their own soil.

Mohr let out a long breath and wondered how he would explain the loss to his battalion commander, Colonel Donner. The old man had made his frustrations clear when Mohr transferred into the unit less than two weeks ago. Listening to the colonel grumble about all the headaches caused by 2 Company had been an eye-opener.

Gunnery scores? Consistently the lowest ranking in the battalion. Third worst in the entire division. Somewhere in the bottom ten for the West German Armed Forces.

No less than three major inspections failed in the last six months.

To top it off, a locker drinking party in January had resulted in an huge drunken brawl that ended with two arrests – both of the suspects were enlisted men from 2 Company.

Five years ago, the poor behavior and low performance rating would have been swept under the rug. That became impossible with the implementation of Army Structure 4. Now there was increased accountability across the board along with higher performance standards and an overall push for training and re-training as needed. Stones were being kicked over from on high and it was time for NATO's conventional forces to address the rot that had set in from the early 1970s.

To that end, Colonel Donner had stared at Mohr with pleading eyes and confessed. "There are big problems in 2 Company. I need you to fix them. Fast."

Mohr then spent two miserable weeks working closely with the company to prepare for this exercise. It gave him a chance to observe the men very carefully. It didn't take long before the problems became apparent. The enlisted men were excellent. It was the platoon leaders that needed a good kick in the rear.

For years, they had been pampered by the previous company commander, Captain Harting. As a result, their egos had grown unchecked and there was an overall tendency to do things the easy way. Training had lapsed and the enlisted men were without positive guidance. While the rest of the army had been quick to take on the new mandate of overall improvement, 2 Company had ignored the memo. Now the wound was festering.

Mohr would have to work feverishly to undo the damage or the division commanders would disband the unit entirely.

If that happened, the men would be scattered to the four winds of administrative hell in the German army. Promotions and choice assignments would elude Mohr for the rest of his career.

The two weeks had rushed by and Donner had made it clear he expected positive results from this exercise. Instead, things had gone bad from the very start. The only thing good to report was that there was still a shred of hope based on today's performance.

Lieutenants Meier, Kessel and Unger had at least grudgingly tried to do what Mohr had proposed in the briefing. Though their platoons bumbled along in sluggish formations, Mohr saw potential. There was no question it would take time to smooth out the bad habits - but he had an idea that might help.

After today, he would give the platoon leaders a refresher course on modern tactics. Since it wasn't always possible to always go out in the field and practice using real vehicles, Mohr would train them on paper maps with cardboard counters. Results would be determined by rolling dice and consulting charts.

It wasn't anywhere close to the real thing, but it would help teach the basics of movement and fire that they had all apparently forgotten.

While the tank crews stretched their legs and smoked cigarettes in gloomy silence, Schmitt's three Leopards rolled down the muddy trail and halted just short of the clearing.

Mohr pushed down the urge to lash out. Perhaps there was some very good reason for the SNAFU - though his mind failed to conjure forth any real possibilities.

"What happened?" he asked, trying to keep his tone free of accusation.

"I told you it was a bad plan," said Schmitt. "Doomed to fail from the start."

Mohr bristled from the insolence. Who did this man think he was? A flurry of rage-filled expletives filled his mouth like cotton candy. With so many choices, his mind failed to select a single one. What fell out instead was a spluttering cough mixed with muddled syllables of disbelief and anger.

The edges of Schmitt's mouth twitched into the slightest of smirks and Mohr caught himself as he realized he was being baited into a trap.

A glance around him revealed its nature.

Kessel, Meier, and Unger were riveted on the scene. None of them looked at Schmitt. Their gaze clung to Mohr, as if they were studying a specimen. Having grown up in a small town, it wasn't the first time he had seen such looks. These faces were reserved for newly arrived outsiders whose every action was under close scrutiny. Instantly, Mohr's perception of the situation shifted like the change of a TV channel.

I am being judged.

One wrong move now could wipe out his chance of ever gaining the respect he needed to do his job. Though 2 Company needed drastic change, it was also true that if he pushed too far and too fast, he would lose just the same. Despite the danger that 2 Company now faced, the junior officers had been slow to accept the reality of the situation.

Schmitt was the worst of them. The only thing larger than his ego was the battalion-sized chip on his shoulder. Instead of seeing Mohr's early attempts to change the company for the better, all he seemed to detect were threats to the order of how things had always been done.

Maybe it wasn't too late. Maybe the man could yet see reason. Mohr took silent measure of the smirk on the lieutenant's face and saw it for what it was - a taunt.

Try to pull rank and see what happens. Do it.

Mohr sidestepped the trap.

"Lieutenant Schmitt, I'd like to have a word with you in private, please. Everyone else, you're dismissed."

The smile on the lieutenant's face withered. Only the glare remained.

Mohr watched the other tanks disappear off down the forest road until the two men stood alone in the clearing. Lieutenant Schmitt took a wide stance and checked his watch as if he were a headmaster awaiting the arrival of a chronically late pupil.

Neither man said a word as Mohr lit a cigarette and took a long soothing drag before he spoke.

"What seems to be the problem, lieutenant?"

"The problem is that you have no idea what you're doing."

"Please enlighten me then." It was time for both men to put their cards on the table. If Schmitt could be redeemed, he needed to know right now. The sabotage and backstabbing had to stop here.

"You don't know these men like I do. Captain Harting knew what it took to lead us. When to push. When to let go. You do not."

"Well, you're right about that," said Mohr. "I've only been with this company for two weeks. I need you to give me some time to acclimate. On the other hand, changes need to be made. Colonel Donner has made that clear enough to me."

Mohr hated to name drop but if that was what he needed to do in order to turn Schmitt from enemy to an ally, then so be it. The job of transforming the company would be so much easier without his stubborn resistance.

"So what do you recommend, lieutenant? I'd like to know," said Mohr. "Speak frankly." It was an invitation as much as it was a dare.

"Quit."

The word shot out like a bullet.

Mohr's world turned crimson until he reminded himself that he told the man to be honest. He asked the junior officer to repeat himself.

"Look, I know you're working very hard, but the men don't respect you," said Schmitt. "And frankly, neither do I. You cannot hope to gain their loyalty. But I know them well enough to lead them."

The words hung in the chill air. In a matter-of-fact tone without a trace of hostility or anger, Schmitt had spelled it out for him and dispelled any illusions of possible redemption. The truth was apparent now. Lieutenant Schmitt was a cancer that needed to be excised. The time for tact was over.

"Lieutenant Schmitt, I'm not going anywhere," said Mohr. "Whether you like it or not, I'm in command of this company by right of rank, training, and commission. From now on, you will obey every order I give to the letter. If you have objections to that, I'm willing to listen in private. But don't you ever question me again in front of the men. Is that clear?"

Schmitt clicked his heels together as though he were back in basic training.

"Understood, sir," he shouted.

The words were slathered in sarcastic tones. Without waiting to be dismissed, Schmitt stalked off towards the Wolf jeep. Its Mercedes engine revved and the gear crunched before the vehicle shot out of the clearing and off down the road.

Mohr was left alone to figure out how to get rid of this man. The answer seemed clear enough. He would crush him with officialdom.

It would take mountains of paperwork and careful documentation. Each of Schmitt's missteps would be written down in detail and submitted as part of an official record. When at last there was enough ammunition, he would request a formal dismissal for the lieutenant.

It would take months. But time was surely on his side

HILDEBRAND AND HADUBRAND

May 1985
Headquarters, 24th Panzer Brigade
Landshut, West Germany

Captain Kurt Mohr stood in the officer's mess hall and rubbed his tired eyes. It was nearing midnight and he would normally be in bed after a long day of training with the men of 2nd Company. Before he could catch a wink of sleep, the brigade commander had ordered all the officers to watch President Reagan's primetime speech to the American people.

The lively conversation that normally filled the place was completely absent. Instead, everyone was glued to the big TV set perched up near the ceiling in the corner of the room. The brigade XO checked his watch and turned up the volume. A Volkswagen advertisement faded out, replaced by the image of President Reagan sitting at his desk in the Oval Office. He wore an expression as grim as a funeral.

In somber tones, he started off his address to the American people, informing them that he was about to reveal the shocking extent of Soviet treachery and lies. His next stern words were directed at the men in the Kremlin. In no uncertain terms, he warned them against taking any kind of military action that might threaten NATO members or American allies around the globe.

"America will honor its commitments to its allies and partners in full," he said.

Reagan then announced that the American military and several private companies had worked together for the past two years to create and develop new software to enhance photographic imagery. The fledgling technology had only been installed two weeks ago on the cameras of America's premier spy plane, the SR-71 Blackbird. During a rare overflight of Eastern Europe, one of the aircraft had taken photos that provided shocking proof that the Soviets had been disingenuous in their recent efforts to foster world peace.

The camera zoomed out and the American president then stood up and pointed to several reconnaissance photos on display next to his desk. The first image was a top-down color photo of a forest just east of the Inner German border. Nothing was visible except for its green treetops. The screen changed to show the same forest but now the white outlines of hundreds of tanks and vehicles were clearly visible underneath its canopy.

"Despite announcing a phased drawdown of its forces from Eastern Europe six months ago, the Soviets have done the opposite," Reagan claimed. "They have been playing a rigged shell game with their army. While one regiment withdraws to the USSR, two more are secretly transported into Eastern Europe by civil rail and air to take its place. In some cases, entire divisions have been disbanded on paper only to be renamed and repositioned in hidden locations near the West German border."

A collective gasp swept through the room. Mohr stood there in disbelief. All signs had shown that the Cold War was slowly winding down. The tensions between the two superpowers had been receding lately. Things weren't perfect but it seemed like the possibility of war was much lower than only a few years ago.

First, the Soviets had surprised everyone by unilaterally withdrawing their intermediate missiles from Eastern Europe. Met with scepticism at first, international teams of military observers had confirmed that they had done it in record time.

Next came the partial withdrawal from Afghanistan. Without delay, the Soviets pulled back a majority of their divisions while leaving a skeleton constabulary force behind in Kandahar to train the fledgling army.

There was even serious talk of relaxing the situation at the border between the two Germanys. And now he was being told that the Russians were planning to invade. It seemed like a sick joke. Was the American president senile?

Reagan finished by stating that under advisement from the joint chiefs, he had raised the alert level of the United States Armed Forces to DEFCON 2 – the highest it had ever been since the Cuban Missile Crisis. Mohr's confusion turned to a sour heavy shock that gnawed at his stomach as the realization set in. He had stumbled into a living nightmare.

The brigade commander stormed into the mess hall and announced all leave was canceled. NATO's colored alert level was now Orange. Such an alert indicated a high probability of an enemy attack within 36 hours. Reams of paper with marching orders were doled out among the officers.

Mohr stubbed out his cigarette and picked up the ink-smeared sheaf of papers that ordered the battalion east towards the border with Czechoslovakia. His tank company was only a small cog in the big wheel of the 1st Mountain Division, but he was determined that it would do its part to keep the West Germans safe from the Red Army.

By 0200, the entire 24th Panzer Brigade was heading east along Autobahn 92. Their mission was to mount a mobile defence of the main roads and highways that would take the Czechoslovakian tanks west over the Danube River, towards Landshut, and onwards to Munich. Mohr's company belonged to the 244th Panzer Battalion, one of the two tank-heavy forces in the brigade.

By the time the brigade had completed its eighty-kilometre road march, Mohr was already drained. Though the men of 2nd Company were exhausted, everyone began the drudgery of digging into their initial positions near the small town of Grafling. Mercifully, an engineering team showed up with a bulldozer to create the high berms from which the tanks could fire behind.

Pits were also dug into the nearby hills for the Leopards to shoot from, their hulls afforded cover by the surrounding ground. The infantry slaved away among the pine trees, digging foxholes and trenches. All around Mohr was a buzz of activity.

Just before sunrise, his tanks and infantry were finally in concealed positions on a hillside, waiting for World War III to begin.

AT THE BREAK OF DAWN

Near Grafling, West Germany

Captain Mohr fumbled with an unlit cigarette when the leaves rustled somewhere behind him in the darkness. He turned to find Hoffman standing there at the edge of the clearing.

"Do you really think it's going to happen?"

The dim pre-dawn light painted the young man's haggard face.

Mohr understood his concern. He had been on alerts many times before but something about this one just felt different. For one, the nearby town had been quietly evacuated during the night. That was new.

There were concerns that the other towns and cities to the west would be evacuated too but the rumor going around was that the German government didn't want to provoke the Soviets further now that NATO had raised its alert level.

After a short internal debate as to whether it was better to tell a comforting lie or an unhappy truth, Mohr went with honesty.

"I don't know but we'd better be prepared for it," he said. "Get some sleep. Today will be a busy day. War or no war."

Hoffman nodded and turned away. Hunched over, he trudged back through the clearing towards the dark outline of the Leopard tank. At a geriatric pace, he slouched under the camouflage netting, mounted the hull, and slid through the driver's hatch.

For the first time since departing Landshut, Mohr was finally alone. How absurd it was to have his daily routine ripped out from under him while politicians debated and men he had never met prepared to kill him.

He gazed down the long gentle slope of the hill. Below him sat the sleepy little Bavarian town of Grafling, just a stone's throw away from the Czechoslovakian border.

If and when war came, he would experience his first taste of it here. Was he really ready for it? His hand shook as he fumbled with the lighter twice more before giving up. He tried to focus in on his thoughts and identify the main source of his anxiety. Maybe then he could eliminate it, like an enemy tank caught in the crosshairs of his gunner's sights.

His mind drifted to the men who served under him. They were flawed human beings, just like he was. Despite what the Hollywood movies showed, enlistment in the military did not automatically bestow moral purity or quality of character upon those who signed up. For every resourceful and hard-working soldier he encountered, there were the shirkers and the idiots to balance it out.

The vast majority of the Heer's members were simply average people who were content to do their jobs each day and go home like in any other organization. Each army was a cross-section of the society from which its members came. The great leveller among all these different people was the training they were given. This was what allowed an army to go about the business of killing and dying.

The tank crews in his company had plenty of training. They had conducted extensive maneuver and live-fire exercises in Shilo, Canada. They had also taken part in annual REFORGER exercises that allowed the NATO forces to work together and practice the tactics they would need to use in the event of a war with the Warsaw Pact.

Of course, there were also the countless hours spent in the simulators at Grafenwöhr, where the crews would run through drills again and again until each action was automatic. After the simulation ended, each decision was then analyzed. The instructors were brutally honest and unafraid to point out every mistake, constantly pushing the crews to work harder and more efficiently.

Morale was not an issue either. They all knew what was at stake. Germany was their home. Their families and friends were here. No one was being asked to fight for any abstract concepts like freedom or capitalism. Conducting a defensive war here was a simple matter of survival – an assertion of the right to exist. They would all fight until they had either won or were killed.

The habits and tactics of his unit were an issue. Mohr was a new company commander who had transferred in only six weeks ago. When he first embarked with the company on a field exercise, the results were less than encouraging.

Some of the platoon leaders had listened to Mohr while others had merely gone through the motions. One of the officers, Schmitt, had taken a sadistic pleasure in letting a group of Americans ambush the whole company and then had the nerve to lecture him. The man was grossly insubordinate and Mohr had been building a case against him for weeks. Unfortunately, time had run out and now he was stuck with the man as they reeled headlong into war.

The other officers showed a grudging willingness to work with Mohr but they didn't see the point of changing their tactics. To them, the best thing to do was to simply park their tanks on the reverse slopes of the hills near the enemy team's objective and shoot. Recent attempts to use paper maps and dice to teach more nuanced methods of small-unit combat were met with mixed degrees of success.

The problems in 2 Company stemmed from years of coddling by Captain Harting, the company commander whom Mohr had just replaced.

From what he could piece together, Harting had taken a relaxed approach to the business of battle tactics. He had apparently thought the main purpose of a tank was to simply sit there and blast away at targets without any concept of maneuver.

These were not the type of tactics that Mohr had been taught at the armor school in Munster. There, he had learned to use decisive and swift movement throughout the battle. The purpose of a tank, his instructors said, was to create not only destruction but total chaos. The former was caused by firepower and the latter was created by movement.

Once the enemy commander was in a purely reactive state, you got inside his decision cycle and ripped him apart.

Mohr had explained these concepts to his platoon leaders and they had intellectually understood them but it was hard to overcome human inertia. The men stubbornly clung to the older and easier way of doing things.

Mohr had no doubt that over time, 2 Company would be transformed into a tank force that employed the latest in armor tactics with great skill. But that time had run out and now they were about to go to war. How could he retrain a tank company in the middle of a war? It seemed crazy to even try it.

The question shifted slightly in Mohr's mind. Would the tank perform in real combat as advertised?

He turned towards his Leopard 1A4 tank sitting silently in the darkness. Designed by Porsche, it was a 40-ton steel beast that he had trained on for the last five years. The firepower of its Royal Ordnance 105mm main gun was impressive but the newer tanks were being upgraded to 120mm. There were loud debates among tankers as to whether the older tank's main gun would be enough to penetrate the armor of the new generation of Soviet main battle tanks.

The Leopard's thick steel armor was supposed to provide its crew a decent level of protection. It was of a previous generation and there were serious questions about whether the armor would stand up to a 120mm enemy tank round. Mohr doubted his tank would survive a hit to the hull side or rear but the turret front armor might survive a round. He hoped to never find out the answer.

The technology inside the tank had been upgraded throughout its twenty-year production span. Mohr's tank had recently been upgraded under the German army's accelerated modernization program. The new fire control system was a tank gunner's dream.

The tank's powerful ballistic computer could automatically adjust the main gun's elevation and movement to ensure a hit on moving targets, even while his tank was moving at the same time. The latest round of tinkering had resulted in a thermal sight being added, which allowed the tank to fight even at night.

The tank commander's PERI system worked much like a submariner's periscope. Mohr could sit safely inside the tank and get a 360-degree view of the battlefield at two- and eight-times magnification. He also had a monitor that allowed him to see exactly what the gunner was looking at.

Mohr could even override the gunner and fire the main gun himself. Although it was quickly becoming obsolete, the Leopard 1 was still a deadly killing machine designed with one mission in mind – destroying Soviet hardware.

Of all the doubts and certainties to consider, the one he worried the most about was himself. Was he ready?

This question could not be answered so easily as the others. He was a newly-minted company commander. Brought in from I Corps up north, he did not have enough time to get familiar with the terrain in Lower Bavaria or the men he worked with.

During his short time here, he had encountered uncertainty from the enlisted men and thinly-veiled hostility from his platoon leaders. There was no way around his inexperience.

Could he really lead this company into war? It seemed like a huge challenge for a kid who grew up without role models of his own. The fifth of seven children, Kurt Mohr had grown up in a turbulent home that lacked in everything but strife and hardship.

Having an alcoholic father who never offered the guidance he so needed was somehow worse than being a child of acrimonious divorce. At least those kids never had to hide under the bed or make up stories about the bruises that materialized every so often.

How was he supposed to be a father figure when he had none of his own? The responsibilities were enormous. Not only was he the commander of his own tank with its four-man crew but he was also in charge of four platoons of three Leopard tanks each.

As war approached, the burdens got heavier. Just before the march east, Colonel Donner had swapped out Lieutenant Meier's tanks in exchange for a platoon of Panzergrenadier infantry commanded by Lieutenant Muller. As if that weren't enough, Mohr was handed a pair of Luchs scout cars, a flak battery of two Gepards for air defense, an M113 mortar carrier, and a pair of Jaguar armored vehicles with HOT anti-tank missile launchers.

The weight bore down hard on Mohr's conscience. All those men out there in the dark were counting on him to make the right decisions. Some of those choices would involve sending them to their own deaths.

He pulled a poncho over his head and lit the last HB of the day. Inhaling deeply, he tried to find some peace within himself. As the small roll of tobacco burned down to its filter, he swore to himself that he would do everything he could to protect his homeland. If he only did that then nothing else mattered.

Mohr climbed in the tank, shut the hatch above him and slept like a baby.

WORRY WORRY SUPER SCURRY

Mohr strode over to "Two One", his company HQ Leopard tank, and opened the commander's hatch. Down inside the turret, Fischer sat at the gunner's station eating a chocolate bar.

The tank stank of hot farts, body odor, and half-eaten MREs. With four men sleeping, eating, and working together in its confines, the stench was more or less permanent. Only the intensity varied. This morning was especially foul and Mohr held his breath as Fischer stared back up at him, his angular jaw moving like a cow chewing her cud.

"I'm heading off to check on Alpha platoon," said Mohr. "I'll be back at 0600. Keep an ear on the radio."

Fischer smacked his lips together loudly. "Yes, sir. But if Hoffman sings that damn song one more time, you may have one less member of the company when you return," he said.

Mohr knew exactly what the gunner was talking about. Moments ago, he had walked right past Hoffman relieving himself against a tree while humming "99 Luftballoons."

"Yeah...we will make do," Mohr replied.

He walked through the trees and light brush that thinned out further down the slope and found his way over to Schmitt's position. The sun had just come up over the hills to the east. Fighter jets high above raced towards the border and turned back west at the last second.

Mohr watched them while he walked, regretting it when his foot caught on a tree stump, sending him crashing to the ground. His knee stung painfully and he swore to himself as he got up and limped the rest of the short journey.

"War hasn't even started and I'm already injured," he growled.

Schmitt's tanks were parked in among a small group of tall pine trees. Draped over them was the camouflage netting that concealed them from the air. Mohr stepped on a branch. Crack! There was panicked movement amid the trees.

A stuttering voice called out.

"Halt! Step forward. Identify and give the password," it said in high-pitched terror.

Mohr froze, racking his brain and hoping he would not be killed this morning by a sentry whose voice sounded like a twelve-year-old going through a rough patch of puberty.

He jarred his memory then shook his head. "Password is Nena. It's Captain Mohr."

After a short pause, Private Berger stood up from his dugout, the MP2 submachine gun levelled at Mohr. "Oh! Captain Mohr," he said. "Pass forward, sir."

"Good job, Private Berger," said Mohr. "Now would you mind perhaps pointing your weapon away from me?"

The sentry looked down in shock at the weapon in his trembling hands. "Oh," he said, before lowering it.

Lieutenant Schmitt stood in the cupola of his tank, pretending not to notice the company commander's approach. When Mohr came within arm's reach of the tank, the lieutenant ducked down inside.

Would the army prosecute an incident of fratricide just before the start of a major war? Mohr's hand tightened on the grip of his submachine gun and waited a full minute passed before Schmitt popped his head up again, like a gopher emerging from his hole.

"You have your men preparing their positions?" asked Mohr.

Schmitt pointed over towards the crest of the hill. "They're over there digging," he said. "We'll be ready."

Mohr bit his tongue at this news. He wanted the men in his company to be fresh and ready for combat if it came – not exhausted from digging in. Schmitt had interpreted Mohr's orders last night in such a way that his men were being treated like slaves. There was also the issue that the men were now out there on the exposed side of the hill. If the enemy saw them, their positions would be reported and they would lose the element of surprise.

"Well, I want you to pull your men off that detail immediately and rest them," said Mohr. "Make sure they're properly fed and relaxed."

Schmitt shrugged. "I was about to do just that."

"Good," said Mohr. "Can I see you for a minute? I'd like to talk to you about why you weren't at this morning's briefing, I'm sure you have a very good reason."

Schmitt ducked back down inside his tank again.

Mohr's patience was at an end. "Lieutenant Schmitt! You come down from that tank right now. That is an order!" He climbed up on the tank and flung open the hatch, half-surprised it wasn't combat-locked. Schmitt looked up, his face clenched in silent rage.

"Lieutenant, dismount immediately. That's an order," said Mohr, trying his best to sound calm.

Schmitt clambered up out of the turret. They both hopped down from the hull into the untamed grass. Mohr looked around to see several of the men in the platoon trying hard not to stare at what was happening right before their eyes.

"Follow me," said Mohr. They walked away from the tanks and down the hill until he was satisfied they were both out of earshot of the men.

"I was so busy that I forgot about the morning briefing," muttered Schmitt.

Mohr shook his head. "You'll see to it that from now on, you'll be at each morning briefing before the other platoon leaders or I'll have you on report." He took out his map and unfolded it. "Now let's go over the plan together, shall we?"

Schmitt stood rigid as a statue as Mohr gave the same briefing as he had given earlier. By the time he had finished, his seething anger had subsided to a dull annoyance.

"Any questions?" asked Mohr.

"No sir," said Schmitt. "If you'll excuse me, I have to get back to my platoon."

"Dismissed," Mohr told him. Schmitt snapped off a salute so crisp that it could only be mocking in its intended effect.

Mohr nodded. "We don't salute out here, lieutenant. The enemy might see that and decide it's a grand idea to blow my head off."

Schmitt smirked and walked back up the hill towards his platoon.

Mohr limped carefully back up the slope towards his HQ tank. Since arriving at the battalion six weeks ago, His relationship with Schmitt had always been tense but today marked a new low.

There was no doubt that the lieutenant needed to go. But doing so now, on the verge of war, would rattle the men and create further division among the officers. He had only himself to blame. Mohr had sensed the problems early on but had decided to bury the man with paperwork instead of shaking things up like he should have.

Now there was was no time left. They were stuck with each other, caught in a dysfunctional relationship.

Mohr cursed and swore to himself as he made his way towards his tank. By the time he returned, he had made his decision. After this alert was over, he would put in a request for a transfer to a new company or tender his resignation. Colonel Donner would have to find another lackey to fix the problems of 2 Company.

Not ten paces from his tank, artillery rumbled off near eastern horizon.

War had come.

THIS IS WAR

Mohr stood in the cupola, his attention glued to the battalion radio net. Even though his tank's newly installed digital radio was supposedly impossible to jam or intercept, Colonel Donner had ordered strict radio silence while the companies were in their deployment areas.

He had also made it clear that Mohr and the other company commanders would only hear whether hostilities had commenced or war had been averted and the alert was cancelled.

It was just as well because hearing anyone talk over the jumble of squeals and white noise on the frequency was impossible. Judging by the scream of artillery shells and the accompanying blasts near the border, it was obvious what was happening.

As of 0600, the men of 2nd Company were at war. It was time to let his platoon leaders know.

The ground underneath Mohr's tank trembled like a fawn in winter. The thunder of explosions continued unabated for two minutes. The men sat silently in the tank until Fischer spoke. "The American cavalry must be getting totally destroyed out there," he said. "My god. This is really happening."

Mohr finished his radio check and cracked his knuckles. The company net was clear of jamming. At the very least, he could talk to his platoon commanders.

"Alright men, hostilities have begun," he said over the tank's intercom. "Let's move with the rest of the company towards our positions and prepare the welcoming party."

Hoffman drove the tank out of the clearing and traversed along the reverse slope of the hill. Mohr called a halt when the tank was one hundred meters to either side of Schmitt's and Unger's platoons. Kessel's platoon pulled in at the very bottom of the slope. Muller's men on the other hill were somewhere out there in their trenches, getting ready for battle.

Mohr wanted to say something brave and inspiring but decided it wasn't worth breaking radio silence. The time for talking was clearly over.

As he waited for the scout reports, the layers of doubt and worry that had consumed his thoughts slid away. Now it was all very simple. They would succeed or they would fail. They would die or they would live. His future had shrunk from an array of vast possibilities to cold steel binaries.

After what seemed like a very long time, he received a radio call from his lead scout troop. "Charlie Two One. Spot Report. You've got incoming friendlies coming west along the highway. Two Mike Threes. One Mike One. ETA one minute."

He nudged the intercom switch. "Hoffman, I want you to drive up towards the crest. I need to see what's happening down there for myself."

The Leopard 1 bumbled up the long spine of the hill, halting just short of where the ground abruptly flattened out before beginning its sharp decline. From here, the tank's hull was still largely concealed. Mohr leaned forward in the turret to look down on the long strip of highway that shot straight south.

Less than sixty seconds later, a pair of battered M3 Bradleys reversed south at full speed along Route 11. One of the vehicles had a series of large dents along its sides. It resembled a soup can that had been hurled down a very long flight of stairs. Behind it, an M1 Abrams tank screamed down the road. The turbine engine whined like a jet fighter.

A wave of brain-stabbing panic enveloped Mohr. The last window of opportunity to run out of here was rapidly closing. All he had to do was climb out of the tank and run as fast as he could.

No!

He fought back against the animal instincts that welled up in his gut. His senses sharpened as he swallowed down his emotions, and banished the fear and panic back to the darkness from where they came. This was his home. These were his men. They would fight and die for it.

A gigantic series of blasts washed over the town of Grafling. Mohr closed the hatch and watched through the PERI as the little shops and houses buckled and collapsed into piles of lumber, brick, and concrete. Pulverized masonry and powdered concrete filled the misty air.

Another round of shelling followed, churning the remains into a morass of gray matter. A grim curtain of murky smoke ascended from the scattered remains. And just like that, someone's hometown was reduced to a memory.

Gut-churning silence followed.

The ground rippled under the tank and the monitor in front of Mohr trembled like a leaf in the wind.

"Dear God," said Hoffman as the baritone grumble of the artillery strike receded. "The whole town. It's just…gone."

"Hang on," said Mohr.

The air above the tank was suddenly filled with the ear-splitting screech of hurtling metal. The first blows came down like a fist on a drum set. The ground under the tank bucked as the artillery splashed down nearby. The Leopard crew rocked back and forth and side to side as the rounds bit at the ground and shards of shrapnel slapped at the tank's armor.

A numb kind of terror settled over each man as the rain of shells spat down on them.

It seemed like at any moment, the ground might open up and swallow them whole. He had never felt so vulnerable in a tank before. Explosions ripped through the air again and again all around him. His monitor flickered on and off, the blasts playing havoc with the vehicle's delicate electronics.

At the expense of a few artillery shells, the million-dollar tank might be rendered completely useless before it had a chance to fire on the enemy.

Lange spoke up. "Sir, we need to get out of here now!"

Rational thought broke through the murky undertow of primal fear.

"Reverse!" Mohr shouted.

He switched over to the company net.

"Alpha! Bravo! Charlie! Get the hell back down the hill!"

Buffeted by the force of hundreds of artillery shells, Two One flew back down the slope and came to a jarring halt at the base of the hill.

Mohr had never experienced anything like it before and wanted so much to never go through it again. He suddenly had an entirely new and real appreciation for the English term "shell shock". Worse than anything was the feeling of being totally helpless, denied even the dignity of shooting back at the bastards who were trying to kill him.

Through his dust-caked vision blocks, he caught sight of his other tanks emerging from the thick wall of dirt that the massive artillery rounds had kicked up.

After another minute, the sick crunching sound of nearby impacts stopped. At long last, the rain of fire mercifully ceased.

Mohr felt like he had just been on the losing end of a bar fight. Fragments of punchy thought emerged from a foggy haze. His heart hammered in his chest, a physical reaction to his terror-stricken mind. Sounds came over his headset but he could piece none of them together into any coherent whole. Fischer stared at him, his jaw slack in a hazy stupor.

Mohr squeezed his eyes shut, trying to summon the willpower to coax his faltering mind back to life. It was like pulling on the recoil start cord of his old dirt-bike - the engine sputtering and dying each time. With one enormous yank, his brain finally turned over. Mohr keyed his radio and asked the scout team for a situation report.

The reply was calm and cool. "Two One be advised. You've got three lead tanks – Tango Five Fives – coming your way straight south towards you down Route 11. I count at least twenty more behind them. Looks like a battalion." The scout gave him further details with map coordinates, speed, and distance. Mohr let the information sink in and tried to take the good with the bad.

He took a breath and spoke simply and clearly over the radio. "Get ready," he told the platoon leaders. "They're coming."

CAULDRON

Mohr took a deep breath and keyed the intercom, his voice trembling and unsteady. Somehow just uttering the words made the situation seem all the more real.

"T-55s coming down the road."

The older tank model hinted strongly that it was the Czechoslovakians coming his way. No matter, he thought. He was an equal opportunity tanker and would gladly service any targets they provided him, regardless of vintage or nationality.

Mohr kept talking to his crew, hoping that his voice would pull the other members of the tank back to reality after enduring the howling storm of artillery fire.

"Alright men, I know you were hoping to fight the Russians today but it looks like we'll have to be satisfied with the Czechs. Their equipment is a bit older but at the ranges we're dealing with, they're still dangerous. They'll probably be using lots of inaccurate close-range volley fire. We'll be well protected in our fighting positions so don't panic if things get hot. Fischer, make each shot count. I want accuracy over speed.

"Hoffman, be careful not to throw a track on the loose gravel near the crest. Alpha will be covering us, so there's no need to drive like you're at the racetrack. I'll be busy on the radio for the most part so everybody remember your training and work as a team."

"Yes sir!" he heard the shouts of his men echo through the tank's enclosure.

Mohr examined the landscape through his PERI sight. The world outside was completely shattered. Where once the hillsides had been green and lush, they were now scarred by violence. Vast smoking craters and shell holes shaped the earth. A gloomy pall of dirt and smoke blotted out the blue sky.

"Pull forward over the crest into our firing position," he told Hoffman.

The tank rolled up the hillside like a boat traveling over the waves as it charged through giant pits smashed into the ground. Traversing the forlorn landscape brought to mind the grainy footage of American astronauts driving around the desolate surface of the moon in their buggy.

At last, the Leopard slowed and nestled just behind a berm. The top of the turret and the main gun barely cleared its top edge. From here, the gunner had a clear view of the valley below.

Mohr surveyed the remains of the ragged forest that covered the hills on the opposite side of the road. The neat rows of pines were now an obscene tangle of demolished timber. The trees that remained were mere suggestions of their original form. They had become limbless poles with trunks hunched at ridiculous angles. It was a perversion. His gut clenched at the sight.

What gave anyone the right to do this to his homeland? Was he worth so little in the eyes of others that he had no right to enjoy it?

Using the joystick, he slew the main gun to the left while watching through the PERI sight at full magnification. Far down the road, he saw the first enemy tanks approach. It was time to answer back to this desecration. He fumbled slightly with the hastily-installed digital radio before tuning it to the company net.

"Echo Two Four. Echo Two Five. Engage," he said.

The pair of Jaguars rolled southeast from their concealed positions near the ruins of the town. Their path followed the gentle curving base of the hill upon which Mohr's tanks perched. A few seconds later, they came to a halt amidst the smoking rubble of a farmhouse and fired. The HOT missiles streaked meters above the valley floor, leaving pencil-thin trails of smoke in their wake.

One of them curved gently off to the right about midway through its flight and slammed into the side of the eastern hill. The other missile found its mark.

An enemy tank erupted in a column of flame and the turret jumped a dozen feet in the air. The round hunk of metal made a lazy pirouette before landing a dozen meters away from the burning hull. Mohr allowed himself the slightest grin.

"Yes!" shouted Fischer. "That tank is gone!"

The remaining pair of T-55s peeled off to either side of the highway. One of them fired wildly in the direction of the Jaguars. The shot burrowed into the ground at least a hundred meters from its target.

The Jaguars responded by unleashing another salvo of missiles. This time, both of them struck home. The lead Czech tank platoon was transformed into a trio of crisp metal hulks. One of the vehicles detonated repeatedly, its ammunition brewing up under the extreme heat of its fiery fate.

"Okay, Echo. Pull back immediately," said Mohr.

The Jaguars turned in a wide clockwise circle to the north. Once they met the highway, they veered south on the road and ran straight through what little remained of Grafling.

Mohr's radio squawked and the faint voice of one of his concealed scout teams deployed far to the east identified himself.

"Two One, I've got eyes on four platoons heading your way in column formation," said the scout. "That's two OT-64 platoons and two T-55 platoons. They're heading straight down the highway."

"Get ready," said Mohr over the intercom. "We have lots of bad guys coming this way. Gunner, hold fire. I want Alpha platoon to deploy on our left flank and hit them first. I'll tell you when to fire. Be ready to move back over the hill as soon as we get a shot off."

"They aren't even going to lay down smoke first?" asked Hoffman.

"Doesn't look like it," said Mohr. "Stay alert though – they might decide to hit us with chemical weapons."

Mohr considered how badly a chemical strike would ruin his ambush plans. The infantry on the other hill would need to wade down through the thick vegetation towards their trenches and fox-holes while wearing heavy and uncomfortable chemical weapons gear.

Then they would need to set up their MILAN launchers, acquire targets, launch the missiles accurately while under fire, and then break down the weapon and trudge back up the slope. In the meantime, they would need to coordinate their fire and movement with each other while trying to communicate through gas masks.

No wonder Muller was unhappy this morning.

Mohr thought of how to simplify his plans. The battle had already started and now he realized just how much he was asking of his men. They were highly trained, disciplined, and motivated. But in the end, they were only human. What looked good on paper now seemed decidedly impractical.

Fischer spoke up. "I see multiple vehicles coming this way!"

Looking through the gunner's sights, Mohr made out a large group of enemy tanks rushing down the road, followed by smaller infantry fighting vehicles with round turrets. These were eight-wheeled OT-64s, similar in shape and size to the Russian-manu-factured BTR-60. As the column of tanks drove straight down the highway, several of the little vehicles parked just off to either side of the road.

After increasing his magnification on the PERI scope, Mohr noticed infantry climbing out the roof hatches of several carriers. No doubt, they were there to suppress enemy armor with anti-tank missiles and RPGs while the rest of their regiment rushed forward.

It was bad news.

With a range of three kilometers, the wire-guided missiles could badly damage or even destroy a Leopard tank. If the infantry got close enough, the rocket propelled grenades would burrow right through his thin rear armor.

The OT-64s had to die.

Mohr slew the turret towards a carrier until the gunner's display matched his own. The crosshairs fixed on the target and the laser rangefinder's digital readout blinked 1900 meters. He adjusted the crosswind velocity and handed control of the main gun over to Fischer.

"Gunner, target the carriers while Alpha is firing on the enemy tanks. Make each shot count! Wait for my order to fire."

"Understood," said Fischer. Mohr heard the young man's nervous stutter but didn't know what to say. The time for reassurance seemed well past.

Below him, the T-55s rolled along Route 11. The Czechs were driving as fast as they could go. As they approached the town, the lead enemy platoons tried to move into a wedge formation but the tanks on the highway would not match speed with those traveling off the pavement. By the time they reached even with Mohr's position, the Czechs were completely out of formation - just a jumbled collection of targets charging headlong towards Grafling like salmon in a rush to spawn.

Mohr keyed his radio set. "Alpha! Engage the tanks immediately!"

Seconds later, Schmitt's platoon rolled over the crest of the hill just to the left of Mohr's position.

The first of his Leopards rolled right past its defensive firing position and stopped inside a small blast crater. Another one sat on the crest doing nothing. Silhouetted against the sky, the enemy immediately focused its fire on it. The ground in front and to the side of the Leopard erupted with the impact of each high velocity round. A missile whipped over the top of the turret and detonated in mid-air a hundred yards past the target.

Schmitt's third tank managed to reach its firing position nut did not fire. Instead, its turret turned left and right as if slowly shaking its head "no".

Despair and outrage tugged at Mohr's insides. He flipped to the intercom and spoke to Fischer. "Gunner! Engage at will! Kill those carriers!"

The Leopard rocked back as the main gun flung off an anti-tank round. The coax spit out a long stream of 7.62mm rounds at the infantry teams that were scattered nearby.

The gunner shouted in excitement. "That's a kill! Loader! SAB-OT!"

Lange jumped into action, removing the expired shell remnants from the breech and shoving in another armor penetrator round.

Mohr watched through his PERI as Alpha platoon lumbered into action. At last, one of Schmitt's tanks fired its main gun. Instead of hitting a target, the shot struck the earth and sent up a fountain of dirt.

"Alpha! Fix your formation!" shouted Mohr.

On the opposite hill, Muller's men still had not managed to fire off a single shot. The tangled mess of smoking vegetation and limbless trees that sprawled over the hillside hinted at the problem. The infantry teams were still hiking their way through the forest towards their firing positions. Muller must have been furious.

Something metallic slapped the outside of the turret, shoving Mohr backwards into his seat. The screen in front of him rolled like an old television set.

"We're hit!" shouted Hoffman.

"It's okay," said Mohr immediately. "We're alright. Just do your jobs." The monitor's vertical hold kicked in again and his screen stabilized.

"Two One. Spot report," the lead scouts radioed. "I have two enemy tank platoons diverted off to the west side of the highway. They're coming over the hills directly towards your position."

The main gun fired again. Fischer claimed another hit on an OT-64. The cheering had stopped now and the crew was working smoothly together as a team. A pair of rocket propelled grenades smacked into the turret. A quick check revealed nothing was damaged.

"Start loading up some HE rounds," commanded Mohr. "Take out that infantry down there."

A quick call over the radio summoned the M113 mortar carrier positioned far to the west. Mohr ordered them to fire alternating smoke and HE rounds down into the growing mass of infantry below. Seconds later, the first rounds crashed down into the valley.

Mohr couldn't shake the cold heavy dread. His ambush was supposed to have been a smooth and practiced operation that would cause total shock among the enemy. Instead, it was clumsy and confused.

Schmitt's men were useless. Muller still needed time to get into position. And now they were about to be outflanked unless he directed Kessel to help out. Things were falling apart!

Mohr gathered his thoughts and got on the radio again.

"Okay, Bravo, I want you to roll out to my right. Alpha, get ready to pull back," he said. "Charlie, I want you to move to our left flank. We have incoming enemy tanks."

Mohr's attention was hauled away by the dull thump of an explosion to his left. Through the PERI, he spotted one of Schmitt's tanks burning. Acrid smoke poured from its turret hatches.

To his right, Unger's tanks poured over the crest of the hill in neat unison. The Leopards reached their positions at the same time and fired immediately. All three shots crashed into their targets. Just like that, a platoon of Czech tanks on the outskirts of Grafling was reduced to flaming scrap.

Schmitt's two remaining tanks raced backwards up the slope and disappeared from sight on the reverse side of the hill.

"Bravo, shift one hundred meters south and get into position. Slow down and find your targets."

Mohr started to wonder if Kessel had heard his order in all the chaos. He nearly keyed his radio again when he heard back from him.

"This is Charlie. I'm in position right now," reported Kessel. "We're engaging two platoons of T-55s at close range."

Schmitt's tanks barrelled over the crest once again. This time, the pair of Leopards stopped short of the berms and opened fire. One of the tanks managed a hit while the other sat there doing nothing.

Mohr gave the order for Bravo to pull back. Unger's tanks reversed back up the slope together in a neat line formation. All his tank platoons were now accounted for – but where the hell was Muller?

As if in answer, a puff of smoke drifted up from the hill opposite of where Mohr sat. One of the remaining OT-64s exploded as the MILAN missile struck and penetrated the vehicle's thin armor.

"Fischer! How are we doing on those tanks?" asked Mohr.

The tank rocked back from the Leopard's 105mm main gun firing downrange. "On the way," said the gunner. His voice sounded more controlled. Mohr felt a touch of pride in his crew, calmly performing their tasks as a coordinated unit after having survived the initial panic and excitement of battle.

"Still lots of them out there, sir," he heard Fischer say calmly.

"Driver! Reverse. Let's get back behind the hill."

The Leopard's engine roared to life. Halfway to the crest of the hill, the tank jerked to a sudden stop. Mohr rolled his eyes, waiting for the next round of bad news to arrive. Hoffman gunned the engine again and the tank jittered and shook as it tried to back up the hill. Instead of the sensation of backward motion that he expected, Mohr only felt and heard the road wheels grasping for traction and the drive sprocket spinning uselessly.

"Looks like we've thrown a track!" shouted Hoffman.

The turret shuddered again. The tank rang like a bell, the vibration of a non-penetrating hit sending shivers through its interior.

"We're hit!" shouted Fischer. "Should we bail out?"

Mohr closed his eyes before he spoke, trying his best to sound calm and collected. The tank was a goner. But it wasn't the absolute worst thing that could happen to them. They could be dead or wounded. This ranked a close second.

"Calm down, men," he said. "Driver, see if you can get us back into our firing position. We're too exposed here. Gunner! See if you can find who's shooting on us and fire back!"

The Leopard staggered towards the nearby berm and jolted to a stop. Its hull sat at a forty-five-degree angle to the slope of the hill. Looking out through the PERI, Mohr could see that part of the tank's hull was exposed. The forward half of the hull jutted out beyond the protective barrier, leaving it vulnerable to enemy fire.

Mohr's options narrowed drastically. He could stay here or try and move again. The former option left them partially exposed. The latter would risk the tank sliding completely out of the firing position. Time was running out. The other friendly tanks were getting farther away from his position as they withdrew south. The tank's gun belted out a round again.

If they stayed here, they would die. It was that simple. They could abandon the tank and try to run back up the hill. It was less than one hundred meters to the hill crest, but the prospect of charging uphill under enemy fire seemed worse than crazy - it was suicidal. The only thing left to do was to bring Kessel's men back and hitch a ride in the Marder.

"Charlie, we're immobile right now and need a lift," said Mohr. "Bring your men back here near our position. We need to bail out. Use our tank as cover and bring the Marder in as close as you can. Get the ramp down and be ready for us. Be advised we're taking enemy fire here so you'll need to suppress."

Kessel replied over the company net immediately. "Hang on. Nearly done here."

Mohr watched the carnage on the valley floor below. At least half the enemy's tanks were burning. None had gotten past the town. Several of the surviving tanks were firing back at where Muller's infantry positions had initially begun to engage them. Enemy infantry teams were running up the hill, firing the entire way. Soon enough, they would find only an empty network of trenches. When that happened, they would refocus their efforts against Mohr's tanks. Time was running out for the West Germans.

Nearly five hundred meters to Mohr's right were Alpha and Bravo platoons, firing and moving together. They would soon reach the last firing position and the ambush would, by necessity, begin its withdrawal phase. Mohr didn't want to think about what being left behind would feel like.

Behind him, Kessel's tanks fired in unison as they raced over the hill crest. They drove within ten meters of his vehicle and took up hull-down positions in the crevices and shell holes around him. The Marder raced towards Mohr's tank and turned neatly before reversing and coming to a halt less than two meters away.

The ground near his stricken tank erupted up as a nearby round exploded. It was time to get out.

"Alright men, that's enough!" said Mohr. "Bail out immediately and get into the Marder behind us. I want you to move as fast as you can! Now go!"

Mohr flicked a switch on his commander's console, releasing the four smoke grenade dischargers. Instantly, the outside of the vehicle was bathed in a cloud of thick gray fog. The hatches flung open and the men clambered to get out of the vehicle.

Mohr got on the battalion net and ordered the M109s to fire the smoke barrage that would cover his company's retreat. He waited for the tank to empty before grabbing a white phosphorous grenade and swinging open the commander's hatch. One of Kessel's tanks boomed from less than ten meters away. Despite having ear protection, his head rang and he felt like his eardrums were being stabbed.

Through the haze, Mohr spotted the Marder sitting right behind his tank. All he had to do was cover a meter or two of open ground. Lying on his side on the rear deck of the tank, he summoned the will to do one last thing before sliding off the turret and running for dear life.

Mohr pulled the pin on the grenade and threw it down the open hatch. Its dull thump sounded just as he rolled off the hull. There was no time to spare a thought for the fiery end of his beloved Two One.

Mohr tumbled towards the ground. A sting of agony coursed along his ankle. He scrambled to stand up but collapsed again on the broken earth. Two pairs of feet rushed past him and disappeared in the belly of the Marder.

Crawling on hands and knees towards the troop carrier, Mohr felt as if he were stuck in a slow-motion nightmare. He paused and looked up at the short distance to the ramp. It may as well have been Mars. There was no way he could get there like this.

One of Muller's infantrymen charged out of the carrier. Two arms wrapped around his waist and grabbed dragged him across the yawning gap. Once inside, he sat on the floor, gasping for breath as the Marder raced up the slope as the ground erupted in its wake.

On the other side of the hill, the Marder slowed and two of the grenadiers yanked the ramp closed. Kessel's tanks formed up in the lead and together, they raced along the reverse slope towards the south. By the time Mohr caught his breath, he noticed he was short one crew member.

"Where's Fischer?" he asked.

"Dead," replied Hoffman.

Lange's tears fell down his filthy face. Everyone else in the Marder pretended not to notice. There was one other issue Mohr had to take care of.

"What's the status of Alpha's knocked out tank?" he asked.

"No survivors," said one of the grenadiers.

HEROD'S LEGACY

The remains of 2 Company sped south down Route 11 and into Deggendorf. Riding in the back of the Marder, Mohr felt a rush of pure adrenaline co-mingled with an intense guilt that he was alive and Fischer was not. Though the elation quickly numbed, the grief gnawed away at him. He summoned the inner strength to banish the raw emotions. It was time to lead his men again.

The Marder halted near the center of the city. Mohr poked his head through the commander's hatch. In front of him, the Territorialheer had opened a roadblock for his men and tanks to pass through.

They wore faces of grim determination as they waved Mohr's vehicle forward. Armed with antique weapons from the last war, they would prove little match for the advancing enemy tanks and they knew it. Yet, here they were - ready to fight and die for the people they loved.

Mohr's heart dropped as he watched the pleading faces of civilians in the windows of homes and shops. The looks of hopelessness in their eyes burrowed into his conscience. Some of them were packing their vehicles out on the street in a hurry, trying to get out of town before the enemy arrived.

Along several side streets, long lines of civilian vehicles sat at the roadblocks. A chorus of honking filled the air while the police and auxiliary forces tried in vain to turn them around.

"Go home!" they shouted. Grudgingly, the cars and trucks inched off to the side to allow the tanks passage.

The Marder sped across the four-lane bridge to the west of the city. Halfway across, the air cracked like a whip. The bridges to the north and south crumbled and plunged downwards into the Danube. It was a sure sign that 1st and 3rd Companies had just pulled back across the river.

"His" bridge – the Deggendorf-Mitte Bridge, was the only one left intact. When everyone crossed over, it too would be blown. The Czechoslovakians would find their progress blocked by the river's deep flowing waters.

"All platoons check in," he called out over the radio. Mohr waited to hear back, hoping that everyone else had made it across. Although they had left the Czech regiment in ruins behind them, the second echelon would arrive soon enough. To his immense relief, the platoon leaders answered.

Schmitt sounded shaken and confused but all his remaining vehicles were on the west bank. The two scout vehicles were the only ones that remained on the east side, still picking their way through the heavy traffic of Deggendorf.

Sure enough, when Mohr reached the west bank of the Danube in Fischerdorf, the pair of Luchs scout cars came into view. The Marder's ramp came down and fresh air filled the inside of the vehicle. The panzergrenadiers spotted the scouts crossing the bridge and cheered them on. Mohr couldn't suppress a smile. He felt glad to have them safe and sound. Once they were across, he would blow the bridge and together they would ride west away from this hellhole.

The scout teams had done an excellent job of reporting the enemy's position. Had it not been for their spot reports, his company's flank would have been ripped to shreds by the enemy's tanks.

The hard lesson had not been lost on him. He had based his plans on the enemy's intentions while ignoring the enemy's capabilities. Mohr's instructors back in Munster would not have been pleased. It was only by luck that they hadn't taken more casualties than they had.

Through his binoculars, Mohr spied the low buildings they had just passed alongside on their way through Deggendorf. Plumes of smoke from the town billowed upwards into the sky as the enemy's artillery began to fall. Time had run out – the second echelon was about to arrive. His gut tightened as two dark specks emerged from the wall of smoke to the north. As they approached, he made out the bulbous shape of the approaching helicopters.

"I've got inbound air!" shouted Mohr. "Helicopters inbound! Bring the Gepards back!"

The two helicopters swooped in fast and low towards the bridge, ripple-firing a salvo of rockets. The bridge shuddered with the impact near its mid-point. A fiery flash enveloped both scout vehicles. Only two husks of metal sat in their place.

One of the Gepards laid down a thick stream of 35mm fire from its twin autocannons as it reversed. The helicopters swung back around to the north, dropping low in a bid to avoid the incoming rounds. Seconds later, they vanished into the wall of smoke from which they had first appeared.

"They'll have reported back about the bridge," said Mohr. "We need to blow it now."

His chest tightened as two men crawled out of the mangled scout car. One of them flopped to the ground as he took his first desperate step towards the west side of the bridge. The other scout picked him up and swung him over his shoulder in a fireman carry.

They were a hundred meters away. The man carrying his friend stumbled and crashed face-first into the pavement. Mohr ducked down into the vehicle and got on the radio with Unger.

"We're heading back onto the bridge to get those two men. If we don't make it, tell the engineers to blow it immediately!"

"Reverse! Get us back on to that bridge," Mohr told the driver. "There are two men out there we need to pick up."

Donner shouted over the radio. "There's a second echelon heading straight towards you. Blow the bridge! Do it now!"

Mohr swore and shouted at the driver. "I told you to reverse!"

The vehicle shot forward over the cracked pavement. Enemy tanks would be here any minute now. The Marder jerked to a halt just a few meters short of the scouts.

Several of the grenadiers rushed out of the hatch and grabbed them. Once they piled on board again, the driver jammed his foot on the accelerator.

The screech of shattered metal filled the air. An enemy tank round bit into a nearby steel archway. Mohr ducked down into the Marder as the shards rained down. When the shower finally stopped, he brought his head back up out of the hatch and scanned the east bank. To his horror, a pair of T-55s rumbled along the roadway toward them.

Mohr screamed down at the driver.

"Go! Go!"

The carrier rushed back west along the bridge. Two of Unger's Leopards blasted at the oncoming T-55s. The Marder, caught in the middle, pressed forward in a straight line towards the safety of the west bank. One of the enemy tanks stopped and shuddered after a round sliced through its front hull armor.

The Marder's treads touched the pavement on the western side of the river. Mohr dared to look back. A stream of traffic swarmed along the bridge's roadway. Among the sea of civilian vehicles were enemy tanks.

Mohr's gut twisted at the sight and a single word fell out of his mouth. "No…"

The throng of harried panicked traffic was nearly halfway across. At least two platoons worth of T-55s drove among them, like wolves running among a flock of sheep. Mohr's Leopards stopped firing at the tanks, afraid to hit the fleeing civilians.

Mohr bit his lip and hoped God would forgive him. The fate of the innocents on the bridge was sealed when he uttered a single codeword into his radio.

"Herod," he spoke bitterly.

A series of charges erupted around the bridge's four large concrete support beams.

The middle span collapsed completely and plunged into the water below. The spans at either end crumbled while the huge solid chunks of twisted iron and roadwork neatly disintegrated in the blast.

The civilian vehicles and tanks plummeted thirty feet down towards the surface of the river. Their impact was marked by a fountains of water. Dark shapes bobbed along the river's surface before they were swallowed up along with their occupants.

The dust of the explosion mingled in the ash-stained air. The company pressed on down Route 92, speeding past the large cloverleaf intersection and interchanges.

Mohr buried his face in his hands, thinking of the civilians he had just sent to their deaths. How would he live with himself? Someday he would make up for it. He promised.

The events of the morning swam through his mind. He was amazed at how complex it was to lead men under fire. The fact that the company had managed to complete its objective at all seemed like a minor miracle.

The strengths and weaknesses of the company were now apparent. Kessel and Unger were solid performers. Schmitt had some cleaning up to do. His coordination of the men during the battle was awful. They had moved slowly and their actions as a platoon had been sloppy. Mohr would ask for a replacement as soon as possible. Enough was enough.

A TANDEM IN TROUBLE

The company's vehicles sat parked around the tree-lined perimeter of a large grassy area near Plattling's city center.

One of Muller's Marders pulled up. Without a word, the ramp lowered and a pair of men dashed out of the back with a crude canvas stretcher.

They loaded up the two wounded scouts from the bridge and rushed them towards the back of the armored fighting vehicle. One of the men screamed over and over. Blackened hands lunged out to Mohr for help. Something caught in the company commander's throat and he looked away. Guilt-wracked and sick to his stomach, he walked from the scene. The wails of agony followed his conscience each step of the way.

Lieutenant Unger walked up and thrust a clipboard full of papers at Mohr. The platoon leader was covered in the grease and filth and dirt of his tank. His fatigues were soiled and his expression no longer held the contempt on display before this morning.

"Sir," said Unger. "I can't believe you went back and got those scouts. I saw it all."

Mohr watched the Marder speed off into town in the direction of the local hospital. "What's our status?"

Unger spoke slowly as if he were forcing the words out. "Seven of nine Leopards are still working. One was knocked out in Schmitt's platoon.

Muller's infantry came back with a couple of wounded. Mohr held up a hand and leafed through the report, trying his best to make sense of the shaky handwriting.

Most of the company's tanks had sustained damage in the last battle. Some of it was as minor as a broken antenna or a malfunctioning smoke grenade launcher. One of Kessel's tanks had even taken a hit to its main gun during the battle on the north side of the hill.

Mohr looked over to see the 105mm barrel bent to the right at a ninety-degree angle. The company's mechanics stopped to admire it before getting down to the arduous job of replacing it.

Over a dozen of Mohr's men were dead. Fischer, his gunner, had been picked apart by heavy machine gun rounds as he bailed out of the tank. One of Schmitt's tanks was blown to pieces, most likely by an anti-tank missile from one of the infantry teams. None of the men could be easily replaced even though active reservists would step in to plug the holes.

The sheer amount of ammunition they had expended was staggering. The company was nearly depleted of its stock of armor-piercing tank rounds. The MILAN missiles were almost totally gone too. What was supposed to have lasted several days had barely gotten them through this morning. They were in desperate need of resupply.

"Where's everybody? I want the other platoon leaders here now," said Mohr. Unger disappeared and returned with Kessel and Muller. No sign of Schmitt.

Mohr was livid. Twice in one day was two times too many. There was no time for the political games and playing nice that had been the norm up to this morning. A raging fire brewed up inside of him.

"Lieutenant Unger, did I not just order you to bring ALL of the platoon leaders here?" he said.

Unger's eyes went wide. "Uh…yes, sir. You did."

Mohr thrust the clipboard back at Unger, the hard plastic edge hitting him squarely in the chest.

"Then where in the hell is Lieutenant Schmitt?" he asked. Unger stared at the ground in silence.

"Never mind. We will all go over to where he is."

Together they trudged towards Schmitt's two tanks. The lieutenant stood in front of one of them, watching his men help the mechanics with repairs.

"Lieutenant Schmitt," shouted Mohr. "Bring your men over here. We're having a meeting."

Schmitt didn't budge. Mohr shrugged and turned to Unger. "Get Schmitt and his men over here. You have thirty seconds."

Unger took off running around the tank, waving at the men to stop their work and shouting at them to go over to where Mohr and the platoon leaders stood. Schmitt wandered up and stood face-to-face with Mohr, his arms folded.

Mohr spoke slowly and deliberately.

"Lieutenant Schmitt, your performance over the course of this morning and the last several weeks has consistently failed to meet my standards," he said. "Not only that, but you have failed to obey orders in a timely fashion. You have undermined the company's ability to carry out its mission. For these reasons, I am hereby immediately relieving you of your duties."

He turned to the platoon sergeant. "Sergeant Hauptmann, you will immediately take command of this platoon. If you feel you are not up to carrying out this task, say so immediately."

Schmitt exploded in rage.

"You murderer!" he screamed at Mohr. "You blew that bridge when there were civilians on it!"

He lunged forward and grabbed Mohr by his throat. Surprised by the sudden ferocity of the attack, he lost his footing and tumbled to the ground. Fingers pressed in against his skin.

Kessel and Unger yanked Schmitt backward, managing to tear one of his hands away. Mohr tried to breathe but no air came into his burning lungs. As he reached towards Schmitt, the world around him turned into a rapidly-closing tunnel.

Tears stung his eyes and Mohr's body stopped responding to commands. He lay there helpless as the world collapsed into darkness. There was a certain irony to surviving an onslaught of enemy tanks only to be strangled to death by one of your own men twenty minutes later. Mohr wanted to laugh but his muscles wouldn't allow it.

The worst part about it all was that Schmitt was right. It was he alone who had made the call. He had sent the code word to blow the bridge and thereby sentenced hundreds of innocent Germans to die in the river. He imagined the bitter clawing death that awaited each car as it filled with icy water and drowned entire families like rats. What right did he have to look down on Schmitt?

Pinned underneath his assailant, Mohr stopped fighting and waited for the end. Instead, the other officers peeled Schmitt away. Mohr gulped as the world slowly came into focus. With the aid of Kessel's offered hand, he stood.

Schmitt writhed and screamed under the weight of Unger and a pair of mechanics. Filled with a sick fascination, Mohr wondered if the man hated him more than he despised himself.

One of Schmitt's men got the attention of a pair of nearby medics, both of whom rushed over to help sedate the former platoon leader.

Mohr wandered away from the scene and walked into the woods by himself. He sat on a large rock and quaked as he fumbled with a cigarette. Finally, he gave up and flung the lighter deep into the woods.

The moment replayed once more in his head.

Did he really need to blow that bridge? Were there any other choices? Or was Schmitt right - he had murdered the civilians on the bridge without trying to find another way first? Perhaps it didn't matter. It was done.

To continue operating at this level, he would need to compartmentalize what had just happened. Later, he would deal with it all – if he were still alive. A cold numbness settled over him like a shroud. What came next was not forgiveness but a sense of shutting off part of himself. Somewhere deep inside, a door was locked and he could never open it again.

Reason slowly returned and with it, came a reassuring stillness. It was Kessel who came to him finally and sat down again next to him, saying nothing.

After a long moment, Mohr stood up.

"Alright, let's get back to work then," he said quietly.

He walked over to the clearing to find his platoon leaders waiting for him, standing at attention. Unger passed the reports to Mohr again, the pages ripped and torn after being flung to the ground during the altercation with Schmitt.

Mohr found the map of the local town with the supply area circled on it. His voice was hoarse and old. "I want all the vehicles to go in pairs to fuel up and restock ammunition. Do it quickly and cleanly. Oh! Make sure all your men get their wounds looked at. No matter how small. That's a direct order!"

As he was about to walk over to the pair of tanks that constituted the remains of Schmitt's old platoon, Mohr heard Private Lange shouting for him.

"Colonel Donner wants to talk to you right now!" he said.

"Where's the radio?" asked Mohr.

"What? Radio? No. He's right over there, sir." Lange pointed to a Wolf jeep that sat directly in the center of the clearing. Mohr gulped. It was a beautiful bullseye for any enemy pilot who might fly over them.

Mohr rushed over to the jeep, glancing up nervously at the blue cloudless sky.

"Sir, I don't think it's safe to -."

Donner reached back and swung the door open. Mohr dived into the jeep and the driver gunned the engine. The sudden turn combined with the acceleration sent him sprawling. They sped out onto the road without pause, causing one of the local police officers to jump out of the way so as not to get run over.

"Problems," grumbled Donner. "All I have today are problems. I need people who will give me solutions. People like you, Captain Mohr."

Mohr sat in the back, saying nothing. He had known Donner a short time, but he already understood that this was leading somewhere. Someone had fumbled the ball and Mohr would have to try to pick it up.

"They're coming across," Donner said. "They secured a crossing site near Straubing. The 245th Battalion tried to hold them but they didn't have enough men to stop them. The Czechs sent in an airborne brigade. They dropped right in the town and grabbed the bridge."

Mohr's throat ached from the fight with Schmitt and speaking was painful.

"We're pulling back again soon," Donner said gruffly. "How are your men?"

"We're ready to move with the battalion," he answered with a pack-a-day voice. "I'll need some replacements from the active reserve battalion."

"You're not pulling back with us," said Donner. "I need you create some space for the rest of us. Give us time to lay down some defenses. Division wants to shuffle the rest of the battalions around. Plug some holes."

The heavy slow-moving traffic thinned out as they drove into the abandoned suburbs. The prim and well-kept little homes served as a stark reminder of a state of normalcy that had ceased to exist as of six o'clock this morning.

Mohr started to worry about his siblings back home near Dusseldorf and wondered if they were okay. He shook his head and brought his mind back to the here and now. Thinking too much about the people he loved was just the sort of distraction that would get a man killed.

A few minutes later, they arrived in the parking lot of a junior high school. It was a three-story building on a little hill in the southwest of the town. Only two days ago, it was full of laughing children with the future opened up wide before them. Now it was where planning took place to help cut short the future of others.

Mohr followed Donner down the dimly lit halls, decorated with paintings and crafts of children. Donner's aide pushed open the double doors that led to the sports hall.

Radio operators sat at school desks that were too small for them. People of all ranks and services ran back and forth. Clerks and technicians in clean crisp uniforms parted like a bad haircut for Mohr, who was covered in sweat and grease and filth.

"This is all for the battalion?" he asked.

"We're sharing this space with the division," Donner grumbled.

He pointed to a corner of the hall where the rest of the company commanders sat snugly at desks meant for adolescents. Mohr felt at ease among their grease-stained faces and tattered fatigues.

He hunched down on a child-sized plastic seat and pulled out his notebook and pen, ready for the day's lesson.

The battalion intelligence officer, Captain Beck, stood in front of them with a map of II Corps area of operation in southern Germany.

There were dozens of pins on the board, each of them showing the rough position of each friendly battalion and enemy regiment. Atop the pins were taped small colored pieces of paper with numbers to denote the nationality and battalion or regiment number.

Mohr marvelled at the number of red pins west of the German border. It was obvious that if NATO was going to win this war, they would need a heck of a lot more blue pins.

"As I'm sure you're aware, NATO forces along the inner German border made contact with the enemy as of 0600 this morning," began Beck.

"In the south here, the 1st Mountain Division conducted defensive operations meant to delay the enemy force's advance to the west until NATO reinforcements arrive. The initial forward position of our brigade's operations was along the Regensburg - Passau axis.

"Our battalion, responsible for defenses forward and to the flanks of Deggendorf, managed to deal significant damage to elements of the 20th Motor Rifle Division, halting its advance east of the Danube. Division was quite happy with our performance.

"However, things didn't go as well in the rest of our division's sector. The 242nd Panzergrenadier and 243rd Panzer Brigades near the town of Cham were hit very hard by the 1st Tank Division supported by rocket artillery and attack helicopters.

"Although our sister brigades inflicted considerable damage on the enemy, both the 242nd and 243rd were forced to retreat southwest. Advance elements of the 1st Tank Division continued straight south down Route 20 towards Straubing, sending a motor rifle regiment along Route 16, feigning an attack on Regensburg to the west. The 22nd Panzergrenadier Brigade deployed near there was ready by that time and had set ambushes all along the highway. It should have been enough but there was one very big problem.

"The 22nd Czech Airborne Brigade had already landed in Straubing before dawn and secured two smaller bridges over the Danube. They captured the nearby engineers and defused the demolitions on the bridge support structures.

"Instead of waiting for reinforcements, the commander of the 22nd Panzergrenadier Brigade ordered half his men off the planned ambushes to go retake the bridges in the city. When the Czechs arrived on the outskirts of Steinach to the north, they outflanked our grenadiers. The commander had no choice but to pull back south across the river.

"The remnants of the three West German brigades are now deployed defensively around Aiterhofen, approximately 20 kilometers to the north of us. We've been sending air up all morning to help them but it's been largely ineffective due to the presence of enemy air defenses. So far, the enemy has halted in the town and is reorganizing there.

"Once they reinforce and resupply, we expect the rest of 1st Tank Division to come south down Route 20 so they can advance west along Route 92 towards Munich. By then, it's a sure bet the 20th Motor Rifle Division will have completed amphibious river crossing operations near Deggendorf. If we don't pull back by then, we'll be trapped. With the Isar River to the south, there will be nowhere left to go."

Captain Franke, the commander of 1st Company, cleared his throat. "The 10th Panzer Division is directly south of us. Can they not send up some reinforcements to help us?"

Beck pushed his glasses up on his nose and answered in his monotone voice.

"The 4th Czech Army sent several divisions south through Austria early this morning. The Austrian Army pulled south into defensive positions in the mountains, preferring to keep their military and neutrality intact.

"Elements of the 10th Panzer Division to the south of us made contact along the Austrian border about thirty minutes ago near Salzburg and Burghausen. The 10th is pulling back its units slowly but they're spread thin. The main effort seems to be a drive straight west along Route 94 towards Munich.

"As you can imagine, we have no one to spare. Everyone is waiting for the French to arrive. The 10th is strung out along Highway 299 from Altotting in the north all the way to Traunstein in the south. Our brigade is pulling back and forming a new defensive line with the rest of the division that covers Dingolfing in the north down to Altotting in the south. The Americans are rushing in an infantry and a tank battalion to cover the area to the north of that. It's not nearly enough."

Donner stood up and handed out a stack of typed paper. Among its pages were the marching orders for the battalion. The rest of the brigade had apparently already moved back to Dingolfing and Landshut and were busy preparing defensive positions.

Mohr flipped through the neatly typed pages and found the table that showed the battalion's companies and assets and departure times. Beside his name, there was an asterisk instead of a number. Such a tiny punctuation mark would certainly mean plenty of trouble for him and his men.

The rest of the company commanders filtered out of the gymnasium and out into the bright early afternoon. Mohr stayed behind to find out more about the asterisk.

"Excuse me, sir?" he said to Donner. He held up the sheet and pointed to the ink-smeared star.

Donner stepped forward with Captain Beck at his side. The middle-aged battalion commander smoothed his thick mustache and cleared his throat.

"The rest of the battalion is moving west as of right now. As I mentioned, we need time to get our defenses set up in and around Dingolfing. You'll take your company north along Route 20 towards Aiterhofen. The enemy is securing the area for follow-on forces to advance down along Route 20.

"Intelligence indicates the 1st and 2nd Tank Regiments are on the way down south as part of the second echelon attack. We want you to get up there and help reinforce the defenses being put by whatever's left of the 242nd Panzergrenadiers. "

Mohr borrowed a lighter from Beck and lit a cigarette before falling back into his tiny chair. The intelligence officer pulled out a map book with a topographical map of the ground around Aiterhofen.

"Colonel Heinrich has reported the enemy advance stalled just south of the town," said Donner. "His Panzergrenadiers are holding the enemy around Aiterhofen. When the rest of the 1st Tank Division arrives, we expect they'll go on an all-out offensive. Without reinforcements, Heinrich's men will not be able to hold."

"I thought you were throwing in air?" said Mohr.

"We are putting in air but taking tremendous losses," replied Beck, as if to a child. "Air defenses are built up all around the enemy sector. We've lost three Tornadoes to heavy anti-aircraft fire while dropping cluster munitions in the area."

Beck dropped a black and white photograph showing several dark shapes located in and around the town.

"The enemy has deployed SA-8 surface to air missiles in the area," he said. "The civilian population wasn't evacuated in time. If we hit them from the air, we'll kill the civilians in the town. If you do happen to find a way to take out the SAMs and the AAA, our aircraft can get inside the enemy's area of operations and do significant damage. I wouldn't count too much on it though. We've been having a hell of a time repairing our airfields after the chemical attacks on them this morning."

Mohr reeled back in his chair. "Civilians!? You've got civilians in there?"

"There wasn't enough time to issue a warning," said Beck. "The remnants of both Heer brigades were ordered to take up defensive positions in the town. As soon as they arrived, they found the civilians already there and refused the order to fight for Aiterhofen. It would almost certainly have meant the destruction of the town and the death of its occupants. Instead, they fell back into the countryside to the south.

"Some of the civilians evacuated in time but reports on the ground say there are still about a thousand people in and around there. Most of them woke up to enemy tanks outside their homes."

"Sir, I'm not sure we're going to make much of a difference up there. We're only a tank company," said Mohr. "They've got an enemy regiment there right now and a division coming up behind them."

Donner nodded. "That's correct, Captain Mohr. As you can see, the area directly south of Aiterhofen is quite flat except for a few small hills. Perfect for tank operations. Your performance near Grafling this morning has me convinced that you and your men can make the difference."

"The primary mission is to delay the enemy," said Beck. "Just like this morning near Grafling."

Mohr dashed out his cigarette in the nearest ashtray and immediately lit another one. "What can I have for this task? I'm short two tanks and two scout cars already."

"You'll get two replacement Leopards and crew members," said Donner. "We'll take them from 3rd Company. I want you to keep Muller's men and the Marders for this mission too. I have a Bo 105 you can use for reconnaissance. I'm going to need one of those Gepards back from you to help beef up defenses."

Mohr shrugged. What good would the helo do with air defenses in the area? This was a total mess. There was so much being asked of him and so little to do it with.

He peered at the topographical maps in front of him. There was little cover for a tank though there were a few low hills to the southwest of the town. He didn't even want to think about the loss of a Gepard. If the enemy threw air at him, he would have only one vehicle and the infantry's hand-held SAM launchers to help him out.

"Where exactly are Heinrich's men right now?" asked Mohr.

Beck pointed to the south of the Danube River near Straubing and drew a large horseshoe-shaped line on the map. The bottom of the "U" was about nine kilometers south of the river.

"They're holding out in several small towns situated on the highways and roads leading south. He has a battalion's worth of mixed infantry and tanks protecting the major routes south. There's about a company each in Rain and Perkam to the west, Salching and Oberschneiding directly to the south, and Strasskirchen to the southeast. Signal intercepts show that the enemy's main advance is aimed straight south down Route 20."

"We could let the enemy come down south and then try to hit their flanks," suggested Mohr.

Donner nodded and patted Mohr on the back. "That sounds like an excellent idea, captain. Why don't you get out there now and start moving your men? Heinrich has taken heavy casualties. They're tired and low on supplies," he said. "They know you're coming so they're counting on you at this moment."

Beck shoved Mohr a crumpled and torn piece of paper with the radio callsigns and frequencies of units operating in the area.

So this is how one is given a suicide mission, Mohr thought. No one barked orders at anyone or attempted to recite any patriotic nonsense. You just get pulled aside quietly, handed a map, thrown a leg of hope, and patted on the back before being thrust back out there to die.

The orderly drove him back towards Plattling in the jeep. On the way, he dedicated his attention to the task at hand, examining the maps as they sped through the narrow streets of the town.

By the time he arrived, the replacements had come in. The battalion's mobilization company was drawn from other units in the brigade to help fill out depleted companies. A new tank was found for Schmitt's old platoon. Mohr received a Leopard company HQ tank and a new gunner in place of Fischer, a nervous boy named Vogel. Unfortunately, the scout cars were gone for good.

An hour later, the men of 2 Company were driving north up Route 20.

HEART OF DARKNESS

They drove north in a long column along the two-lane highway of Route 20 towards the town of Oberschneiding. The thunderous clap of artillery grew deafening as they approached. It was the soundtrack to entering a giant all-consuming maw that would accept nothing less than their total destruction. Having the experience of being directly under a barrage, Mohr shuddered at the thought of going toward another one.

Down inside the armored turret, he felt more like a passive bystander than a company commander. Still, he could see everything he needed through the vision blocks and the PERI. Anything was better than being turned into minced meat by the knife-edge shrapnel of a lucky artillery round.

Numerous attempts to contact Colonel Heinrich had failed. Mohr was left to consider the grim possibilities. Either the man was already dead or enemy jamming was simply throwing up too much electronic fog for his digital radio to penetrate. Either situation would pose problems for his company.

Occasional bursts of static and high-pitched squeals filled the radio net as they got further north. Mohr gave up after the hundredth failed attempt to reach him. If he wanted to contact the man, they would have to talk face-to-face.

Unfortunately, Beck's intelligence was hours old and he wasn't even sure where the friendly defensive positions were situated - or if there were any friendlies left.

Mohr made a call to the helicopter pilot that circled low above the rear of the column. Thankfully, the company net worked just fine at such short ranges and the little Bo 105 sprinted forward then made two very low passes to the south of what was left of Obserschneiding.

As it pivoted to return towards the company, anti-aircraft tracers from somewhere to the north skimmed inches over its tail rotor. The pilot banked hard and dipped the bird a dozen feet above ground level before returning back south to safety. A pair of skids nearly tapped Mohr's turret as the 105 raced over his tank.

Ten seconds later, the scout pilot calmly radioed back the coordinates of the Panzergrenadier defensive positions. They were located just to the north of Oberschneiding. Without radio communications, however, there was no way to know the colonel's exact location. In order to talk to the man and coordinate the defense around Aiterhofen, Mohr would have to get out of the tank and track him down.

To say he didn't relish the task was an understatement. Enemy mortar fire fell in dribs and drabs over the fields to the north. A mix of friendly and enemy wrecks littered the ground ahead.

"Are you really going to go out there, sir?" asked Lange.

Mohr put his combat helmet on and fished out the submachine gun. "Unless you have any better ideas, then yes," he said. "Make sure you give me a nice burial, okay?"

He hastily deployed the rest of the company into a vee formation behind a slight elevation near the roadside. He dug out the map and showed Hoffman the coordinates that the helicopter scout had pointed out.

"Let's get this over with," he ordered. Hoffman put a heavy foot forward and the Leopard tank bumbled over the uneven ground.

Mohr peered through his PERI as they passed through the chest-high rubble of Oberschneiding. The town was a shattered mockery of its former self. The beautiful old homes were nothing more than burnt-out shells, mere suggestions of their original form.

A gas station, of all things, remained unscathed. "Hey captain, should we fill it up?" shouted Hoffman. Mohr didn't bother to reply.

The tank bumbled into the fields to the north, passing among the destroyed vehicles. Bodies of West Germans and Czechs were strewn like litter over the flaming metal heaps.

Mohr had the distinct feeling of walking through a graveyard. The eerie silence was broken by the firing of a main gun somewhere off to their right. The remnants of a Marder less than two meters away burst into flames as an enemy tank round sliced into it.

Someone was out there. And they were not friendly.

"That was close," said Hoffman. The Leopard's engine hummed as the tank picked up speed.

Before he could tell his driver to slow down, the forward section of the tank dropped. The engine groaned as the ground rose up towards him.

"We're going in a ditch!" shouted Hoffman.

The tank paused and teetered backward on the lip before the hull bowed again. Mohr smacked his head on the panel in front of him, relieved he had already put on his combat helmet.

The tank twisted slightly and then slithered down the hidden embankment. Their progress down the slope was slowed by Hoffman stamping on the pedals to reverse the vehicle. Mohr grabbed the control stick and turned hard, rotating the turret left in an attempt to keep the main gun from getting impaled in the soil at the bottom of the trench. Finally, the tank came to a halt, nearly ninety degrees from level ground.

Hoffman pressed the gas but the tank sat in place as the tracks fought for traction. Mohr closed his eyes and prayed. If he lost this tank, it would be two vehicles gone in one day. He wasn't sure how he would explain that to Colonel Donner - or the rest of his company for that matter.

"Driver! Get us moving!" he shouted.

The engine spat out a grease-drenched wail and the tank lurched forward. It pivoted and settled with its tracks finally resting on the solid ground of an irrigation ditch.

Mohr looked straight back and ahead through the vision blocks to find a way out. Behind and in front of him, the trench curved slightly.

He had no idea how they would get out of here. The walls were just slightly higher than the top of the turret.

"Screw it," said Mohr. "Driver, go straight. Just go very slow."

The Leopard ambled through the ditch with mere inches of clearance on either side of the hull.

Mohr stood up to look out of the hatch. Just ahead lay a group of soldiers, side by side in neat rows. He called out but none moved. A look through his binoculars revealed that several of the men were covered in blood-soaked bandages while others had tarps or blankets covering their heads.

"Cover me with the coax," he told Vogel.

Mohr crawled out of the tank. The painkillers he had been given back in Plattling were working well now. He could barely feel anything as he limped over to where the wounded men lay.

About halfway between his tank and the men. Mohr caught a flash of movement to his right. He turned with his submachine gun at the ready and squeezed the trigger. The weapon made a stubborn series of clicks.

The man who crouched above him looked at him with pure terror in his eyes. "Don't shoot! I'm a medic! On your side!"

Mohr turned back towards the tank and waved his arms, afraid that Vogel would cut the young man down. When he was satisfied that his gunner wouldn't shoot, Mohr spoke up.

"I'm looking for Colonel Heinrich. Do you know where I can find him?"

The young man jumped into the ditch and started replacing the blood-soaked tourniquet tied just above a grenadier's elbow.

"Not far," he replied. "About one hundred meters northeast. Look for the jet. He should be there. If you can't see him, just follow the shouting."

Mohr nodded and turned to go back to his tank before pausing. "How can I get my tank out of here?"

The medic pointed to his left. "The ditch ends over there. There's a little ramp. It comes back out into the field."

Mohr nodded. "Would you mind moving your wounded so I can get the tank through?"

The medic rolled his eyes.

Mohr turned back to the tank and waved. The crew climbed out and carried the wounded around the edges of the tank.

Mohr clambered up out of the ditch for a look north. His senses were assaulted by the scale of destruction all around him. It was like a glimpse into hell itself.

To the northeast, a Tornado fighter jet lay crumbled on its side, having apparently augured into the field at a shallow angle. The passage of the wing through the soil had sliced a deep groove into the earth.

A pair of soldiers squatted behind the berm. A Pioneer tank with a blade attached to the front shoved a heap of soil at them – an attempt to improve the makeshift fighting position. Enemy tank rounds flew past the tracked engineering vehicle, landing just short or slightly to either side. Whoever was driving that thing was either crazy or stupid.

Mohr took a deep breath and belly-crawled towards them. The automatic weapons fire chattered just ahead of him. One of the men in the trench turned around to see Mohr and waved as if they were old friends.

He scrambled forward past the limp bodies of several Panzer-grenadiers, strewn here and there throughout the pockmarked land. The stench of death assaulted his senses and Mohr's stomach rebelled. When he finally reached the grenadiers, his face was a gray pallor and he wished to be anywhere but here right now.

A filthy colonel with grey hair and a dark mustache held a radio headset cradled between his shoulder and his ear. Beside him lay the headless body of a Panzergrenadier corporal, his skin burnt to a crisp.

The battalion commander put down his headset as Mohr introduced himself. Over the din and rattle of automatic weapons fire and explosions, he had to scream to be heard.

"You're from 244th Panzer Battalion? I'm Colonel Heinrich. Thank god you're here!"

"How can we help you, colonel?" bellowed Mohr.

"They sent nearly a whole battalion towards us an hour ago and they fell back. By God, we killed them!

They've been probing our positions since then. Keep your battalion here. I'll ask my other two companies to cover our flanks to the northwest and northeast."

The conversation paused as the Pioneer tank pushed another load of soil up along the lip of the berm. When it reversed, one of the enemy tank rounds finally found its mark. The big vehicle shuddered to a stop. Four crewmen climbed out of the tank and ran to the shelter of the long berm.

"Sir, there were no battalions sent up here," said Mohr. "There's just my company. How can I help?"

Heinrich's grin melted. "Company?" he spat. "They only sent a tank company here? Are you kidding me?"

He turned away in disgust and resumed talking on the radio. "Hold damn you! I said hold! Target that tank!"

Mohr risked a look around the edge of the berm. A hundred meters straight north of them, a weapons team in a shallow foxhole fired off an anti-tank missile. It curved gently to the left in a graceful arc before the operator corrected its trajectory and brought it right.

A half-second later, a T-72 nearly a kilometer away flashed as the warhead impacted its turret and burrowed through the tank's armor. Jagged shards of metal scattered away from where it had hit. As if to broadcast its death, a column of flame leaped up through the commander's hatch.

"We'll need to fall back soon," said Heinrich. "Our scouts have reported two regiments on the way down here. You might make yourself useful by cutting into their flank as we move south."

Mohr nodded and pulled out his map then scanned the terrain with his binoculars. A series of low tree-covered hills to the south offered enough concealment for his tanks.

"What if you pull your men down here just south of these hills along Route 20? We'll hit them as they come down?"

Heinrich snatched the map away from him, gave it a cursory glance and then nodded. "You do whatever you see fit, captain. Either way, you've got about ten minutes before we call in smoke and pull back!"

Mohr checked his watch. Ten minutes was an impossibly short amount of time. He would have to hurry.

AN INSOLUBLE PROBLEM

Mohr crawled back over the hundred meters of muddy ground and burning tanks with the smoke grilling his lungs and watering his eyes.

He avoided looking at the bodies around him everywhere though in truth he wasn't sure he felt much of anything anymore when he saw them.

That scared him more than the bodies.

He slid back down into the ditch and found his tank. His men had just finished moving the wounded and dying out of the way. Mohr grunted a thanks to the medic, who was too busy to even acknowledge the company commander's return.

Mohr climbed down into the tank and sat there trying to picture how the upcoming battle would go. If he were the enemy, where would he go? What would he do?

The area to the west of Aiterhofen was hilly and the roads were narrow. The way east took them away from their objectives. The flat ground to the south straight down Route 20 was the only logical choice, wasn't it?

First, they would send the remaining troops down and try to probe the defenses. Then they would focus all their firepower at one point and pour the fresh men and vehicles straight down into the hole. The enemy wasn't hard to predict but that didn't change the fact that Mohr and the ragtag defenders were outnumbered and outgunned.

When the other three men had slid into their positions in the tank, he closed the commander's hatch and sunk down in his seat.

"Alright, we need to rejoin the company right now," said Mohr. "Hoffman, move back southwest as fast as you can. Don't stop for anything. This time, watch out for sudden drops."

The tank ran up the slope and out of the ditch. The roar of battle outside seemed dim from within the metal cocoon of the tank's thick armor. The tank traversed the bumpy fields and arrived back at the company's main position a few minutes later. By that time, Mohr had formulated a basic plan.

After quickly summoning his platoon leaders, he briefed them on the deteriorating situation up north on Route 20.

"Our friendlies are close to collapse and there are signs that a second echelon is about to come rolling through here to attack again," Mohr said. "We'll take on the first echelon, which should give Heinrich enough time to prepare his own defenses further south."

He pointed to the nearby low hills.

"I want Hauptmann's platoon up there on the east side ready to ambush the enemy as they come south along the highway. The two Jaguars will pull back about a kilometer away. As the first echelon comes down, fire off your missiles towards the rear vehicles when we start shooting. Hauptmann's tanks will take out the vehicles in front. Hopefully, they'll come running south after us."

He jabbed a finger at Kessel and Unger. "Remain concealed on the west side of the hill. When we start pulling back, swing around towards the north in a clockwise fashion. You should be able to hit their rear as they move forward. We're the anvil. You're the hammer. Got it?"

"Once the first echelon is taken care of, we'll see if we can advance up to Aiterhofen before that enemy division arrives and try to take out the air defenses in the town. Maybe we'll get lucky."

Unger looked down at the map and leaned back. Mohr sensed the silent disapproval. This time, he would address it right away. No more skeletons would hide in 2 Company's closet.

"Is there something you wanted to add?"

"The first echelon shouldn't be the problem, sir," he said. "They're likely tired and their ammunition is depleted. It's all the fresh troops coming right after."

Mohr shrugged. "That's true. If we can hit the air defenses, that should go a long way to balancing the odds."

"And if not?" asked Unger.

"Then we fall back with Heinrich's men and make a last stand, lieutenant."

A grim silence swept along the hot wind.

Mohr climbed into his Leopard. A high-pitched whistle signalled the arrival of the first friendly artillery rounds to the north. A gray wall of smoke plumed outward, covering the battlefield in gloomy fog.

He watched the friendly retreat through the little monitor in front of him. Slaved to the gunner's thermal sights, the monochrome view revealed the locations of each of Heinrich's remaining men falling back south along the highway.

In small groups, they ran back towards the steep ditch that Mohr's tank had nearly gotten stuck in. Once there, Muller's Marders pulled up near them. The wounded were loaded on first then the rest of the infantry boarded. All the while, each of the squads took turns firing back through the thick smoke.

One of the Milan weapons teams managed to kill a T-72 at three hundred meters as it made lazy circles around the open field to the north. Heinrich's men were proving themselves excellent fighters so far. Muller would work well under him.

Mohr hoped that other enemy tanks would appear in his sights. If they wanted to try something so incredibly foolish as a blind charge to the south, he and the tanks in Alpha would lay a pasting on them.

A minute ticked by, however, and there was nothing going on but the harried loading of men into Marders before driving south at great speed. When the smoke finally thinned out, only the empty charred landscape was revealed.

Unsure of who or what was coming towards him now, Mohr radioed Kessel in Charlie platoon, hoping they had reached their positions.

The Bo 105 hovered behind the hill where Mohr's tanks lay in wait. Slowly, the helicopter floated upwards until the pilot could barely see over the crest of the hill.

"Spot report. I have eyes on enemy tanks and carriers," said the pilot. "I count two T-72 platoons and two BVP platoons heading straight south down the highway. Approximately a kilometer northwest of your position. You should be able to see them in about a minute."

Mohr broadcast the warning to Alpha.

"Affirmative," replied Hauptmann.

His voice sounded steady and controlled over the radio. What a relief that Schmitt was no longer in charge of the platoon. Hauptmann moved his tanks around with a calm ease that Mohr envied. Alpha's tanks had simply driven up the hillside, found the nearest hull-down positions on the ridge, and sat there echelon right, ready to shoot and move if needed.

The smokescreen had largely dissipated by the time the lead enemy tanks arrived in Mohr's line of sight. The white outline of a T-72 moved through the crosshairs of his PERI, followed by two more of the enemy tanks.

Mohr knew all his men had practiced this scenario a million times in the simulator. Everyone would hold fire and wait for the main body to arrive. Yesterday, he would have prayed that no one got too excited and fired off too early. Now they were all battle-hardened.

He didn't even consider picking up the radio. Mohr just held his breath as the tanks came even with his position, seven hundred meters away. The enemy rolled forward, loosening quick inaccurate fire at the Marders who were baiting the trap.

The next three T-72s rolled into view followed by three BVPs. One of the infantry carriers traveling near the highway failed to spot the steep ditch and drove straight into it.

Its front end slammed into the ground with its rear in the air. The tracks spun in a futile attempt to get unstuck then gave up. Hatches swung open and the infantry stumbled and fell out like a clown car at a circus. Mohr chuckled to himself and then brought the turret over to the lead tanks.

"Gunner. Target front. Tango Seven Two. Engage the target and then take out the lead tanks," he said.

Seconds later, the Leopard's main gun discharged and a T-72 jerked to a halt. A series of short sharp flashes lit up near the ammunition compartment as the tank's rounds exploded. None of the crew left the wrecked vehicle.

On cue, the Jaguars unleashed hell at the rear vehicles. The HOT missiles sprinted over the flat terrain and then slammed down into the thin top turret armor of each main battle tank that trailed the main body.

Four shots. Four kills. The Jaguars pivoted and raced back down south. Mohr's tanks fired a volley and raced off the hill.

The trap entered its next phase. The Marders withdrew into the cover of a forested hillside. Hauptmann's Leopards made a lazy circle to the south presenting themselves as a tantalizing target. Now out for blood, the T-72s shifted their attention to the West German tank platoon and shot wildly at the retreating armored vehicles. None of their rounds found a target.

The three tanks of Alpha platoon, however, scored hits on the move from ranges of five hundred meters. Unlike the enemy, the Leopard gunners took their time to line up their targets. The 105mm gun stabilization was worth its weight in gold.

By the time the rear enemy vehicles entered the final phase of the trap, they were bounding forward in clumsy leapfrog tactics.

Too little. Too late.

Bravo and Charlie platoons rounded the west side of the hill and sped north, wheeling out behind the advancing enemy. Kessel and Unger's tanks sliced through the T-72s and BVPs, cutting through their ranks with ease. The enemy commander apparently had lost complete control by this time as all semblance of formation was lost.

Vehicles veered left and right like a stampede of cattle from a wildfire. Enemy tanks crashed into one another or reversed straight into the gunsights of the two platoons of Leopards.

Kessel and Unger showed excellent coordination with their tanks, firing from a long echelon right formation. One platoon fired while the other moved forward a hundred meters.

Their fire pattern worked neatly from the outside in, bracketing the enemy vehicles with accurate short-range shooting. There was no break in the rhythm of fire - only a steady drumbeat of explosions and flaming metal death that rumbled across the field. By the time the Leopards completed a half-circle, the enemy's destruction was near total.

It was not enough. Mohr wanted all of them.

Two of the T-72 tank crews realized what was happening and turned west in a bid to flee towards the nearest hill. Mohr ordered Hauptmann's men to move along with the tanks to prevent their escape. Both enemy vehicles were killed as they made a futile run up the long slope.

At the sight of the lead tanks getting systematically pulverized, the BVPs pulled back north in a panic. One of them reversed its course back through the field near Oberschneiding. It fell rear-end first right into the same ditch that Mohr's tank had dived into earlier.

Mohr nearly laughed at the sight of it. The ditch had scored two more vehicle kills than most of the enemy tank gunners had that entire morning. He wanted to thank whatever farmer had decided to build such an extensive drainage system.

Kessel and Unger hit the unfortunate BVP with a pair of shots that nearly split the vehicle in two. The black smoke curled upwards from the wreck.

Before Mohr could rest, the Bo 105 pilot came back on the radio with a spot report.

"Looks like you're clear all the way up to Aiterhofen," he said. "No sign of enemy activity to the north yet."

"This is our chance," Mohr told his platoon leaders. "Let's get up to the town, take out the air defense systems and see if we can get the civilians out too."

The tanks raced north back up Route 20. Having a good familiarity with the drainage ditch by now, Mohr reminded his driver to avoid its location.

A few minutes later, they were less than a kilometer south of the town. On the outskirts lay a scattering of small older houses amid newer developments.

The major thoroughfare was simply a line of small shops on either side of the highway.

Five hundred meters south of the town, Mohr ordered his tanks to turn east and run through the open fields while scanning the streets and roads for any sign of enemy presence. He desperately wished he hadn't lost the two scout cars earlier in the day.

Right now, they were losing valuable time as the enemy came towards them from the north. He could risk his tanks and go in the town but without infantry support, they would be extremely vulnerable to any garrison left behind. Mohr cursed to himself.

Why hadn't he insisted on bringing some of Muller's men up here? It was too late now. They would need to try and spot the SAMs and AAA vehicles from here.

It didn't take long until they found one. Private Vogel stopped his scan and declared in a triumphant voice. "Got it," said the gunner. "SA-8. Sitting right near a gas station."

Mohr ordered the tank halted. Peering through his PERI as it was slaved to the gunsight, he saw the target right in the crosshairs. Between a pair of fuel pumps, the squat vehicle sat immobile.

"Okay, let's hit it," said Mohr. "Loader. SABOT. Gunner. Target that SA-8. Take your time and line up the shot."

Mohr rocked back slightly from the gun's firing. The shot hit the chassis, causing the vehicle to tumble on its side and erupt in flames. The gas pumps exploded, sending an angry red fireball up into the air. There was no time to celebrate. The Bo 105 pilot spoke up.

"I've got what looks like two entire tank regiments moving towards here from the north," he said, a quiver in his voice. "Estimate contact with lead elements in three minutes.

Mohr shook his head. All too soon, the next echelon had arrived. Aiterhofen could not be saved.

"Okay, it's time to go then," he said. "Let's pull back."

Mohr's platoons wheeled around and drove back south down Route 20. His heart sank. So much of his plan had depended on taking out the air defenses and rescuing the civilians trapped in the town. Now he felt suddenly foolish for even attempting it.

As his tank pulled into the rear position of the column formation heading south, he felt a stinging sense of failure. The ambush had worked but he had taken too long. Even after they had won the battle, he had insisted on destroying the panicked enemy stragglers.

He was learning all the lessons too slow. Each time he did something right, an obvious misstep showed itself. He had trained with and learned from the best but there it was - the gap between training and real-life experience was always there.

As they crossed over the drainage ditch a third time, Mohr heard his radio come alive. "Helicopters! Six o'clock!"

FIRE AND FLAME

Mohr's tanks scattered as the ground nearby erupted from the impact of rockets. The pair of Mi-8s behind them were in hot pursuit, swooping down over Aiterhofen and coming directly south for them.

Lange threw the hatch open and fired back with the MG3 light machine gun. With little cover in the area, Mohr's only hope was to make a run towards Heinrich's infantry where he had left the Gepard.

He cursed himself for sending the anti-aircraft gun south along with the Muller's grenadiers. In this war, the speed of technology and machinery pelted humans with more decisions than anyone could process in a reasonable time.

So far, the war had been a chaotic jumble of fire and death rather than the precision battle he was trained to expect.

"Make yourself a hard target for that helo," said Mohr to Hoffman.

The young driver grunted an affirmative and swerved the tank left and right, hoping to throw off the pilot's aim.

Through his PERI, he watched as one of the Mi-8s came to a halt and hovered before firing off a Swatter missile from under its wingtip.

Mohr screamed out. "We got a missile incoming!"

The Swatter appeared as a little dancing light in the sky, quickly covering the distance between the firing helicopter and its target. Hoffman's driving grew erratic, jolting the crew from side to side. Mohr lost track of the missile's path and closed his eyes shut, bracing for impact.

The explosion thundered just behind him. He turned to look out of the vision block. One of Hauptmann's tanks erupted in a shower of flame and smoke.

"Keep the fire up at those helos!" shouted Mohr to Lange.

The light machine gun on the turret clattered off a dozen rounds in less than a second. The chances of taking down a helicopter were slim but the fire might be disruptive enough to throw off the pilot's aim.

Mohr watched the sky and tried to piece together the pattern of attack. Flying in pairs, one helicopter herded the tanks with rockets and Machine Gun fire while the other took its time, lining up their aim carefully for the manually guided anti-tank missiles to find their targets.

A stream of explosions raked the ground near Alpha. The other settled into a hover. He stomped and gestured at the huge floating machine.

"There! Fire at that second helicopter. It's going to shoot!"

The Hip fired off a pair of missiles but this time, the enemy helicopter had been too close to the tanks. The pilot was forced to swing away from the stream of machine gun fire. Both missiles splashed into the ground short of their targets.

Mohr looked outside and saw the gentle rise of hills that marked the new defensive phase line where Muller and Heinrich's men were digging in.

"Go straight!" he told Hoffman. "Drive straight down the highway."

The Leopard's treads found traction as they reached the pavement. Perhaps sensing the trap that lay in wait for them, the enemy helicopters circled far away, trying to get more distance from their prey before firing again.

As Mohr's tanks rolled between the tree-covered slopes, both Hips settled into a hover. From a kilometer away, they were little more than black dots against the pale blue sky.

"Get as close as you can to those trees and pull into cover," he told Alpha.

One of the missiles landed near Hauptmann's command tank while the other smashed into the nearby trees, sending jagged wooden splinters crashing through the nearby woods. The helicopters pivoted and fled north. What had happened?

Mohr wasn't sure if they had run out of anti-tank missiles or if the pilots had spotted something they didn't like. Either way, the danger had passed. Sweat poured from Mohr's face and he felt the tension in his muscles ease.

The grenadiers further up the hill fired a pair of missiles at the departing helicopters. The Redeyes shot upwards, reaching Mach speed by the time they were halfway to their targets. The Hips broke off their formation. Now it was time for them to try and stay alive.

The helo on the left released a series of bright flares from the sides of its fuselage. The missile ignored the decoys and exploded moments later, the brilliant fireball consuming its target.

The other helicopter dove towards the ground to avoid the oncoming missile but the Redeye continued on its course, following along with its target. The missile detonated only a meter away from the tail rotor, sending thousands of fragments into the body of the aircraft.

Mohr swore to himself. Had the Hips radioed back their position on the hill? It had to be assumed. His Leopards had survived only at the expense of leading the enemy right to Heinrich's defensive positions.

He radioed for Muller and Heinrich. Both men appeared, red-faced and barely able to contain their own anger.

We have to assume they know where we are now," Heinrich said. "We'll have to move quickly. There's a smaller hill to the south of here. It doesn't offer much cover..." He pulled out a map and stabbed his finger to show the position.

Mohr got the message loud and clear. He knew he had messed up but what else could he do?

Did Heinrich expect him and his tank platoons to just give up and die out there?

The Marders loaded up with troops and reversed down the slope on the way towards a small town flanked on either side by a pair of low hills. Sure enough, the infantry's old defensive position was obliterated by a tremendous burst of artillery fire.

Mohr radioed over to the Bo 105 pilot operating over to the west, asking for any sightings. "I've got at least a regiment across the bridge right now," he said. "They have another regiment waiting to cross. I count forty-three Tango Seven Twos heading south down Route 20. They will be at your position in approximately five minutes."

As the hill to the north was pulverized under a sheet of high explosive firepower, Heinrich motioned to the air control officer, who was busy talking on the radio.

"Be advised, we're sending in air to hit Aiterhofen to suppress local air defenses. We'll hit the enemy as they come over the bridge."

"Negative, there are civilians still in the town," said Mohr.

Heinrich spoke through gritted teeth. "My orders are to destroy every tank coming south," he said. "If that means hitting a town then that's what I'll do!"

Mohr's heart sank. He had failed to take out the enemy air defenses in Aiterhofen and the people there would be punished for it. The town would be pummelled from the air. A pair of Tornado jets screamed in low from the south.

As they got to the outskirts of Aiterhofen, he braced himself for the fireball. Instead, the jets split off from each other and circled back south. A pair of SAMs followed one of the jets and it dropped a series of bright yellow flares while twisting and turning at low altitude.

The missiles slammed into the side of a hill as the Tornado skimmed over its crest and then dipped back down to treetop level, hugging the terrain as it disappeared south.

"What's happening out there?" demanded Heinrich. "The pilots turned back!"

The air controller shrugged. "They won't hit it."

Heinrich's eyes lowered in defeat. He looked like a boxer that had gone down in the first round. "That settles it," he muttered. "We're all dead then."

Mohr wasn't so sure. He scanned the map for possibilities.

This morning near Grafling, his ambush had been made on a set of faulty assumptions. He had based his plans on the enemy's intentions rather than their capabilities. If he had sent out Kessel early rather than holding him in reserve to defend his flank, 2 Company would all be dead by now.

He measured the enemy's potential. Could the enemy send a second force down through the narrow roads and hilly terrain to the west of Aiterhofen while at the same time trying to punch down Route 20 to the south?

Certainly! The enemy commander had two entire regiments at his disposal.

Mohr whipped out his binoculars and spied the sharp rise of terrain marked by the low jagged rocky hills to the west. It was perfect for hitting the enemy as he came down the narrow roads and tight curves that characterized the local terrain.

If the enemy didn't come down that way, the twisting road led right back to Aiterhofen. Mohr could simply direct his tanks north and they would come out on the enemy's flank as the Czechs drove southward. There was no question it could be done. The only issue was how many Leopards would be needed to pull it off?

A quick discussion of the plan with Heinrich followed.

"Do what you want," he replied. "I'm out of ideas."

Mohr shouted over to Hauptmann, who stood in the commander's hatch of his tank, scanning the northern horizon.

"Stay here with Alpha," he shouted. "I'm taking Unger and Kessel west of here. I might be able to hit their flanks."

Hauptmann nodded. If the young man was confused or shocked by the captain's sudden decision, he showed no sign of it. Mohr felt more than ever he was making the right decision. He switched on the intercom and spoke up.

"Driver, I want you to reverse immediately and head southwest through the fields. You'll hit a road. I want you to get on it and go as fast as you can."

Kessel and Unger's six tanks immediately pulled back off the slope with Mohr and headed in the same direction, using the hills as cover from enemy recon units that were undoubtedly positioned somewhere to the north.

Once the tanks had travelled two kilometers along the rough patches of farmland, Hoffman found the road and the tank got up to speed.

Minutes later, they had found the perfect spot for an ambush. It was a high ridge that overlooked a long flat stretch of road with high steep hills at either end. After quickly explaining the new plan, Unger and Kessel got into their tanks and waited.

They didn't have to wait long. While the lead regiment reached Muller's kill zone five kilometers to the east, the Bo 105 pilot reported that another regiment was being sent over the hill to the north of where Mohr and Unger's men waited.

From the cover of the ridgeline, Mohr watched as the enemy artillery crashed into the woods on the valley floor. When it was over, the first enemy tanks would reach the crest of the hill.

Then Mohr's Leopards would pounce.

STORM AND STEEL

Captain Mohr stood in the cupola of his Leopard tank, watching the enemy artillery plunge into the woods to the south.

The Czech commander had made a good guess as to where the Germans were hiding but he had obviously underestimated the long-range accuracy of western tank guns. Had the battle occurred thirty years earlier, Mohr would have had no choice but to put his tanks there.

"Wait for it, gentlemen," he said into his headset. "I want you to drive forward when I give the signal. But don't fire until I give the order."

Unger's tank platoon sat behind him completely still, like predators patiently waiting for their prey to arrive. The enemy barrage pounded the trees at the end of the valley. Mohr winced at the thought of being caught by it. Each thunderous quake was a reminder of his stupid mistake at Grafling.

After several minutes passed, the enemy artillery mercifully ceased. The dust and smoke thrown up by the churning earth and trees lifted. What had been a small green peaceful copse of pines and light brush was now a sick collection of charred splinters of burning wood.

Mohr held his breath and waited for the enemy tanks to show up. Though his static ambush tactics reeked of Captain Harting's tactics, he had to admit that there were times when maybe it wasn't such a bad idea for a tank to remain stationary and blast away at the enemy from long range, if the opportunity provided itself.

At eight times magnification, he had a clear view of the large steep hill that stood two kilometers to the north of where his tanks were positioned. As he expected, the first platoon of three T-72s shot over the crest and rumbled down the slope in column formation. By the time they reached the valley floor, the enemy tanks were bustling along at top speed. Their tracks bit into the grassy land and kicked up a cloud of dirt that marked their trail.

When they met the narrow road, the tanks continued south at full speed. Mohr and his men watched and waited in silence.

The squat T-72s sped along, their turrets stayed straight forward with the commanders buttoned up inside. It was as if they were on a Sunday drive, totally unconcerned about the possibility of an ambush. Soon enough, they would learn their mistake.

Mohr slewed the turret to follow his target and overrode the gunner's sight, showing Vogel exactly what he was looking at. When he was satisfied, Mohr flipped his radio to the intercom and spoke.

"Gunner. Target! Tank. 10 o'clock. Range two thousand. Track it and wait for my order to fire."

Vogel gazed through the sight and replied, the words spilling out just a bit too fast.

"Roger. I have the target. Waiting."

As the lead tanks came nearly even to where Mohr's Leopard sat concealed among the scrub and brush of the ridgeline, two more columns of T-72s descended the slope to the north. The BVPs came next, speeding behind the main battle tanks.

Without any anti-tank missiles, the smaller vehicles posed little threat but the T-72s could indeed do some damage if they managed to coordinate their fire on his position.

He keyed his microphone and spoke to Unger standing by in the nearby Leopards.

"Platoon Bravo, on my order, take up position beside me on the ridge in line formation. Hit the tanks first then go for the carriers."

The teeming mass of enemy vehicles rolled across the floor of the valley. Just as the lead enemy tank column had nearly made it around the bend, Mohr spoke calmly into his radio.

"Now. Move."

The Leopards behind Mohr's command tank roared to life. Seconds later, there was one tank to his left and two more to his right. The latter was just a little too far forward, the front of its hull undercarriage jutting over the ridgeline. Mohr guessed that the driver had gotten too excited. He thought about correcting him but there was simply no time.

"All tanks. Engage!" Mohr shouted. "Gunner. Fire!"

"On the way!" Vogel replied.

The Leopard's main gun belched and the tank rocked slightly with the recoil. Seconds later, the round found its mark, punching into the enemy tank's hull side. The T-72 shuddered and stopped in its tracks. Mohr heard the Leopards beside him join in as they fired their main guns.

"Gunner! Engage at will!" shouted Mohr. "Work your way around the perimeter to the interior."

He ducked back down into the tank. It was time to talk to Kessel. He changed frequency on his radio, hoping that the jamming wouldn't be too bad.

"Delta Three One, bring your tanks around to the north and then swing east behind Hill 221," he said. "You should find the command group somewhere there."

The radio crackled and buzzed before Kessel's reply burrowed through the static.

"Delta Three One to Two One. Acknowledged."

The reply sounded faint and distant but Mohr was sure that Kessel's platoon would perform as ordered. If not, he would probably not live long enough to know about it.

Mohr's tank jerked as its main gun fired again. He was about to open the commander's hatch to get a better look at the enemy position when he heard a loud metallic clang on the turret. "Gunner! Target whoever is firing at us!"

He threw open the hatch and surveyed the carnage on the valley floor. Smoldering and burning tanks and APCs littered the ground as if a careless god had simply flung heaps of flaming metal trash to the earth. The enemy tanks took cover behind the wrecks and fired back. Mohr nodded.

It was time.

He pulled out his map and dialled in a new frequency. "Fire Mission! Fire Mission!" he called over the radio. "Request Fire Mission Alpha!"

Mohr smiled a little, knowing that Heinrich's 155mm self-propelled artillery guns about ten kilometers to his rear would soon be firing on the pre-plotted coordinates. Twenty long seconds later, the barrage of dual-purpose chemical munitions rained down in the middle of the enemy formation.

The effect was instant. The BVPs and T-72s burst open as the artillery rounds sliced through the top armor of the enemy vehicles. Caught under the onslaught of the fire, several of the enemy tank crews panicked and attempted to bail out of their vehicles. As they did, the munitions caught them, ripping them apart limb from limb with fragmentation or incinerating them outright in the blast.

Mohr shook his head in disbelief at the carnage.

"Missile! Incoming!" It was Unger in the tank to his left, screaming over the radio. Mohr watched the smoke trail drift off from somewhere near the northern hilltop.

"Reverse! Get back!" shouted Mohr. The tank bucked as Hoffman slipped into reverse gear and stomped on the accelerator.

The Leopard to his right didn't budge. Mohr saw the treads spin uselessly at the earth, fighting for a grip that just wasn't there. An instant later came the flash followed by the searing heat of a nearby explosion. Mohr's hands shot up to shield his face as he slipped down into the turret.

"I saw it. The missile team is over by that clump of trees near the top of Hill 221," reported Unger.

Mohr checked his map and picked up his radio. "Fire Mission! Shift fire to coordinates…" He realized he was shouting but he no longer cared. One of his tanks was gone and someone had to pay.

At least there was no enemy artillery...yet. If Kessel's tanks didn't hurry up and take out the enemy command vehicles in the rear, Mohr would have to move off the ridge.

"Let's roll up slowly again to the edge," said Mohr. "Keep an eye on that AT position on our left. If you see anything, call it out and we'll pull back right away. Keep firing on the enemy tanks in the valley."

The DPICM artillery fire ceased as Mohr's tank and Unger's two tanks returned to their previous firing positions. The valley had become a sea of fire and death. He scanned carefully for targets hidden amid the scorched remains of dead vehicles.

Vogel found another target and fired. The soil on the face of the ridge below Mohr's tank burst from the impact of an enemy tank round.

Mohr keyed the radio and spoke. Where on earth was Kessel?

"Platoon Bravo, report your position, over."

There was no answer - only static and interference as he called again and again.

Ten seconds later came a fuzzy reply that sounded as though the speaker was underwater.

"We are on the east side of Hill 221 now. Engaging multiple targets," he said. "I think these are the command vehicles."

"Good work, Bravo," answered Mohr. "Keep working your targets. Watch for enemy AT missiles. When you're done back there, swing around and help us clean up the remaining troublemakers down in the valley."

Mohr ducked up from the hatch, his head spinning. In the space of thirty seconds, he had felt anticipation, excitement, despair, and elation. He lifted the binoculars and watched the hillside to the north. A faint wisp of smoke puffed up from a clump of trees.

"AT missile again! Get back!" shouted Mohr. Unger's tank reversed from the edge of the ridge. Mohr's tank didn't move. He keyed his microphone frantically.

"Driver! Pull back now!" he shouted. The wire-guided missile was almost halfway to his position now. Mohr's brain screamed at him to get out of the tank.

His Leopard jolted forwards and back, clearly stuck in the soft soil below. Hoffman screamed back at him. "I'm hung up on something!"

Vogel slew the turret left in the direction of where the missile had been fired. It was nearly two kilometers away but the tank's round hit squarely among the small clump of trees where the crew was concealed.

The incoming anti-tank missile made a corkscrew trail then plowed harmlessly into the base of the ridge. Mohr's Leopard finally found the traction it needed and moved backward.

Over the top of Hill 221, Mohr saw movement and raised his binoculars to get a better look. He was greeted by the beautiful sight of Kessel's three tanks pouring fire down from the top of the hill at the surviving enemy tanks below.

A few minutes later, he surveyed the battlefield. An entire motorized rifle regiment lay in complete ruins before him.

The valley, so very serene and peaceful before today, was now a ribbon of black pockmarked earth. A thick blanket of dark smoke clung low to the ground. The occasional explosion marked the sound of ammunition cooking off in ruined tanks.

Kessel offered a situation report. Music to Mohr's ears.

"We're clear of targets. No casualties."

He sighed and leaned back against the cupola. Unger stood in the hatch of the Leopard to his left. The two men nodded at each other. No bright smiles. No victory cheers. Just survival.

The radio chirped with Hauptmann's voice and the bad news came through loud and clear, like it always did.

Mohr sighed and called over to Unger.

"They're falling back south," he said. "Heinrich's men can't hold."

THINGS FALL APART

Mohr called over to Unger in the nearby tank, explaining the latest development. Just a minute ago, he had heard Hauptmann's voice fighting back the panic as he shouted to be heard over the chaos of heavy close combat.

"Heinrich's pulling his men back south," Mohr said. "It looks like they got hit by two regiments instead of just one. They've taken heavy casualties. Hauptmann's lost a tank. They can't hold."

Kessel's tanks arrived back at the ridgeline. The short squat lieutenant leaned out of his hatch, a far-off look on his face. "We killed them all," he said. "They tried to run when we came around the hill but we gunned each and every one of them down."

Mohr nodded. "Good work. It's time we moved on their flank. Heinrich is pulling back fast. His men are nearly broken."

The six tanks swung up the little road, back towards Aiterhofen.

Near the town, they found them.

Several field artillery pieces sat parked in the barren fields. Their guns were elevated skywards. Mohr took a grim satisfaction in finally being able to return the favour of being shelled by such behemoths at Grafling.

"Gunner! Target those guns! Fire!"

The armor penetrating rounds split the guns apart. None survived. By the time the firing stopped, the artillery pieces were nothing more than hot burning steel.

One major road led into town from the west. Once it reached the outskirts of the little town, it split off into three smaller streets. Mohr shook his head, knowing that any infantry there could pose a huge problem for him. But there was no other way.

"Kessel, you take the north. Unger, go south," he ordered. "I guess I'll take my tank right up the middle. Go as fast as you can."

The tanks sped towards the town as a group and turned off one by one down the narrow streets with rustic little homes lined up on either side.

"I've got a vehicle straight ahead!" shouted Vogel.

Mohr put his hand up to shield his eyes from the sun. In the middle of an intersection were four men with rifles slung over their shoulders. They were standing by a squat OT-65, smoking and laughing.

None of them seemed to pay any mind to the 40-ton tank approaching.

As Vogel adjusted the main gun to line up the shot, one of the men finally noticed that the lumbering vehicle coming their way was definitely not friendly. He turned to say something to the other nearby soldiers just before the 105mm gun blared.

The enemy recon vehicle disintegrated as the HEAT round slammed into it. The four men lay scattered on the ground amidst the pieces of charred metal debris that lay scattered on the roadway.

Mohr heard several other explosions further east in the town. His tank continued forward, shoving the burning jeep's chassis out of the way as if it weren't even there.

To his left, several enemy troops took cover behind the corner of the brick town hall. They squatted together in shock and terror as a tank from Unger's platoon fired its coax machine gun at them from somewhere up ahead. Mohr ordered a halt.

"Vogel, get the coax on those men near the building! Come on!" he shouted.

The Leopard's 7.62mm machine gun spat out nearly a hundred and sixty rounds in less than ten seconds. The enemy soldiers were cut down before they even had time to react. The bodies lay heaped together in death as Mohr's tank rolled forward.

One block further east, something whizzed by the top of Mohr's tank. The second floor of the nearby bank burst outwards and the building's facade rained down on the street.

Mohr turned the PERI around. A flash of movement betrayed an enemy presence to the rear of the tank. At twice magnification, there appeared a helmeted face around the corner of a nearby flower shop. The figure leaned over and propped up an RPG on his shoulder. Mohr used the joystick to bring the turret around and selected the coax.

The first rounds slammed into the brick surface of the building, knocking chunks of it to the pavement. Before Mohr could adjust his aim, the enemy soldier ducked back around behind the corner of the building. "Damn it!" he shouted.

"I've got an RPG team taking cover down the street," he said. "Anyone have a sighting on it?"

No response.

Mohr kept the main gun pointed towards the corner. Hoffman accelerated the tank, pulling further down the street.

"We've got a HEAT loaded!" shouted Vogel. "You want me to shoot?"

Mohr thought about the civilians in the town. The last thing he wanted to do was fire the main gun in the middle of a populated area. There was no telling who or what he would hit.

For the second time in the afternoon, he cursed at himself for not bringing an infantry team with him into town. They were tempting fate sorely by bringing a tank-only force into a built-up area.

"Negative," he told Vogel. "Hold your fire with the main gun. Engage only with coax. I'm handing it back over to you."

Mohr released his grip on the joystick. A moment later, he heard one of his tanks firing.

"I've got a pair of ZSUs here on the east end of town," shouted Kessel. "We're engaging right now!"

Mohr ordered Hoffman to circle around the block, hoping to catch the RPG team before they caught him. It felt like a game of cat and mouse and Mohr was definitely the cat. Without being able to fire its main gun, however, the tank felt more like a cat that had been declawed by its owner.

"Lange, you're not doing anything useful," he told the loader. "Get up there on the MG."

They turned the corner to find no sight of the enemy. The Leopard drove on slowly down the quiet street. Mohr's frustration sunk in deep. Though it was much safer to be in the turret with the hatch closed up, the PERI offered a very limited cone of view. If he didn't get out there and take a good look, the tank would be easy prey for an ambush. He threw open the commander's hatch and stood up.

The tank rolled by a small supermarket on one side and a three-story apartment building on the right. Over the rumble of the tank's engine, he heard a short sharp whistle from above.

Looking up, he saw an older man lean out his window and frantically point in the direction from where they had come. Mohr swung around in his cupola and slapped Lange, who brought the machine gun around.

Not less than fifteen meters away, two men were crouched in the middle of the street. One of them had an RPG launcher resting on his shoulder.

"Shoot! Shoot!" screamed Mohr. Lange tried to fire but nothing happened. Too late, he realized he had forgotten to rack the bolt.

The rocket shot out of its launcher and headed straight towards the rear of Mohr's tank. It went inches wide of the Leopard and struck a street light pole ten meters to the tank's front, knocking the metal pole to the ground over onto the street.

Lange fired the MG, spewing a stream of rounds at the team as they ran off. Within seconds, the pair of Czechs lay on the ground in pools of their blood. One of them spasmed violently for a few seconds before he stopped moving.

The RPG gunner's hands clenched and unclenched as if he were trying to grasp for the weapon that lay just out of his reach. Gradually, the clenching slowed, the man coughed out a stream of pink blood then died.

Mohr looked around the deserted streets for any signs of enemy activity. Nothing stirred. Glancing up at the windows above where his tank sat, the curious faces of the town's citizens appeared, eyes fixed on his Leopard tank.

The radio sprung to life with the measured crisp sentences of the Bo 105 pilot who circled far to the north.

"Be advised you have another regiment heading south across the bridge towards your current location."

Hauptmann spoke next. "Heinrich's ordering the M110s to hit Aiterhofen as the follow-on forces arrive," he said. "You'd better get the hell out of there!"

Things were happening too fast again for Mohr. Not only was he dealing with an oncoming regiment but now he had an impending artillery strike that would kill every civilian in the town.

"I'm near the highway," reported Kessel. "I have eyes on enemy supply trucks heading south on the road. Do you want me to engage?"

"Negative! Get back here!" Mohr answered. "We need to get these civilians the hell out of here."

Mohr looked up at the faces of the families that peered at him from behind the windows of homes and shops. He wished he had a megaphone to call out to them. Instead, he waved towards them and shouted.

"You need to go! Get out of here! Head southwest."

After a moment of hesitation, the door of a nearby shop creaked open and an elderly couple hobbled out towards them. This sparked a flood of townsfolk who ran out into the street. Many of them carried hastily-packed suitcases that they threw into nearby parked vehicles.

Mohr called over to Kessel. "It's time to move out. Disengage! We're escorting the civilians southwest. Get back on the road we came from."

He got down from the tank and found a young adult couple, piling their belongings in a Volkswagen Golf. After a shocked greeting, He laid out the basic plan for them. "Follow my tanks southwest. We're going to Landshut. Don't stop for anything." When he returned to the tank, the radio net was full of voices. Mohr spoke to Unger, wondering why his tanks still hadn't arrived in town yet.

Unger replied in shouts. "I've got enemy tanks coming south from across the bridge!"

"We'll need time to get these civilians out of here," Mohr said. "Do what you can to delay those tanks from coming down here."

He knew his orders were being followed when he heard the thundering blast of a main gun firing to the east.

Thirty seconds later, Mohr and Kessel's tanks were scrambling southwest along the narrow hilly roads, passing by the flaming remnants of the enemy regiment that he and his tanks had destroyed less than an hour ago. The civilian cars kept careful distance from the wreckage. The going was incredibly slow in places where there simply was no room to maneuver.

Kessel's tanks had to pair up and push the destroyed vehicles to the side of the road before the civilian convoy could continue.

Unger reported in. "It looks like we've got an entire regiment coming down here again," he said. "I'm down to one tank here. I don't think I can hold out much longer. Call in some air. Let's take out that bridge."

It was the last transmission Mohr ever heard from the man.

Minutes later, a pair of F-4 Phantoms shot over Mohr's head, flying northeast towards Straubing. The laser-guided Paveways they carried found their target, leaving two giant gaps near the center of the structure. Its steel beam supports were twisted from the force of the explosive power and the southern section of the bridge heaved under its own weight and then gradually collapsed utterly.

It was too late, Mohr knew. The enemy was swarming straight down Route 20, now reinforced by whatever force had made it across the bridge in time.

As Mohr and the civilians proceeded several kilometers to the south, he heard back from Hauptmann. "We gave them a hell of a fight. But we're in full retreat now," he said. "Heinrich is dead. We've less than a platoon of grenadiers. I've lost both my tanks. The Gepards are still here."

The battle was finally lost and the enemy was streaming down Route 20. Mohr's only hope was that they had delayed the enemy long enough for the battalion to secure the defenses around Landshut.

With only five total tanks remaining, his company was less than half its original strength. There seemed little point in taking more losses.

It was over already.

"Okay, pull back towards us with whatever you have remaining and meet up with us," said Mohr. "We're escorting these civilians out of here."

THE BOOK OF EXODUS

As the convoy snaked through the hills, Mohr scanned around him.

The civilian traffic was moving slowly in some parts, quicker in others.

As soon as one bottleneck was resolved, another appeared up ahead. It was tedious work and turned what would normally have been a short thirty-minute drive southwest into an agonizingly frustrating and glacial effort.

The men in the tank were exhausted and, except for Hoffman's occasional grumbling about the civilian drivers, unusually quiet.

Knowing that an entire enemy division was moving all around them was enough to make Mohr keep a constant vigil on the near-by hilltops. If they were spotted by anyone, he wasn't sure how he could respond. He really didn't want to get into a shooting match while his tank waded through the midst of civilian cars packed with families.

The skies began to clear above him as afternoon turned to dusk. He leaned back against the cupola and let his senses take a break from the constant state of vigilance he had enforced upon them since this morning.

All around him, the flock poked its way down the road, gradually gaining distance from the enemy tanks.

Two small children who sat in the backseat of the little car in front of Mohr's tank smiled and waved at him.

A little stupid grin formed on Mohr's face. He had always liked kids but was too scared of having his own. After going through the hell of his own upbringing, he worried that his father's propensity for drink and physical abuse was partly genetic in nature. For that reason, he had avoided commitment of any kind and simply stuck to himself for the most part.

Now, however, here were these sweet little kids he was protecting and the thought washed over him that maybe someday, when the war was over, he would settle down and make a family, avoiding all the mistakes his father had made with him.

As he sat there daydreaming, the car next to him blared its horn. The traffic around Mohr's tank suddenly accelerated. An old battered truck slammed into the back of a newer sedan, turning the hapless vehicle on its side as it spun towards the edge of the pavement.

The couple in the front seat crawled out and rushed to the side of the road to get out of the way of the surging traffic. The other civilians were enveloped in near-panic, trying to squeeze their vehicles through the gaps between cars in front of them.

The once orderly procession was quickly spinning out of control and Mohr had to wonder if any of the drivers even knew why they were all suddenly panicking.

Then he saw it.

Two hundred meters to his left, perched on the crest of a nearby hill were the silhouettes of two combat vehicles.

Alarmed, he brought his binoculars up to get a better view. The turret of his tank traversed towards where he was looking. Vogel spoke up. "Unknown vehicles! Three o'clock. Engage?"

Mohr squinted to try and identify what kind of vehicles were up there with the sun at their rear. Switching to thermal, the PERI revealed the shape of a Marder and a pair of Leopard tanks.

"Negative," said Mohr. "I think that's Hauptmann and whatever's left of Muller's men."

A short discussion with Vogel confirmed that he was indeed looking at Hauptmann's tanks.

Unfortunately, there was no way of telling the civilians that the vehicles on the hill were friendly. The panic only seemed to heighten as Hauptmann's vehicles made their way down the slope towards the convoy.

"Pull back," ordered Mohr. "Get your tanks back and join in at the back after all the cars have gone. You're creating a panic down here."

Hauptmann did as he was ordered and brought the vehicles back up the slope and reversed over the crest.

By the time the frenzy had quelled to a manageable level, the damage had already been done. The traffic was completely stopped, locked together as cars jostled for space to move on the narrow road. Mohr was forced to send Lange and Vogel into the sea of cars to try and direct the vehicles and get moving again.

"What a nightmare," said Lange. "This is going to take hours."

The men got to work. Mohr scanned up ahead for the major bottlenecks and found one a hundred meters ahead.

Three cars and a large truck had collided. The cars were badly mauled along their sides and the truck was overturned. An huge man with a gash on his forehead rushed towards Mohr's tank, beckoning him to come.

Mohr got down from the tank and ran through the tightly packed traffic. As he neared the site of the accident, he heard the awful screams of people trapped inside and pinned underneath the big vehicle. He stood in front of the accident scene, surveying the wreckage and shaking his head.

It was going to take time to get them extracted safely. Time they didn't have. If the enemy caught them here, they would all die very quickly.

"We need to get things moving again," Kessel shouted.

Mohr pointed to the wreck. "Well, we can't just leave them here."

The truck reminded Mohr of a giant wounded beetle stuck on its back. As they approached, the shouts grew louder. The stench of gasoline filled the air and chunks of metal lay scattered on the highway surface.

Mohr and Kessel walked around the truck. The roof had caved in but he could see through a little twisted opening into the cab. Two small terrified eyes peered back at him. Caught in the beam of his flashlight was a wisp of a little girl with abrasions on her forehead and chin. Beside her was a woman who was obviously in shock, crying out her husband's name again and again.

"For the sake of your child, please calm down," Mohr said to the woman. "We'll get you out of there soon."

He checked the jagged hole between the crushed roof and the door frame. There was not enough space for even the child to crawl out.

"Come on! Let's try to open these doors!" he shouted. Several of the tankers started yanking at the truck doors, working them back and forth on their creaking hinges.

The little girl inside the cab began to panic and scream. The damaged doors refused to open wide enough. Mohr gritted his teeth and turned to Vogel.

"Get the tow cable out. We'll hook it up to the doors and pull them off with the tank."

His gunner nodded and ran off towards the Leopard. Mohr tapped his foot and tried hard not to think of the unseen enemy that drew closer with each passing minute.

"Sir, we really need to get going," said Kessel. "If we get caught out here…"

Mohr sighed. "Yeah, I know, lieutenant. Get back to your tanks. If something happens, drive like hell with the civilians."

Kessel disappeared and Mohr watched as his Leopard worked its way around the wreckage of the accident and then backed up towards him. Lange clamped one end of the tow cables to the Leopard's rear deck. Vogel fastened the other end to the truck's door.

Mohr motioned for Hoffman to drive forward. The cable became taut and the door swung open with a yawning screech before separating completely from the vehicle's body.

Carefully, the crewmen of both Leopard tanks hauled the family out. With the help and direction of a pair of nurses in a car behind them, they triaged and began to treat the family. The child had only a few scrapes and bruises while the woman's arm was clearly broken.

The father, however, was dead, having suffered severe trauma to his head. Once it was clear that there was no more that they could do, Mohr got back into his tank, ready to resume the journey.

Just as Mohr's Leopard moved forward, a high-pitched whine filled the air above them. Far ahead of the convoy, a fat ground-attack aircraft swooped low and slow over the convoy and then turned back west over the hills.

He had the distinct gut-gnawing sensation of a mouse that had just been caught by the biggest and baddest cat in the neighborhood.

Mohr scrambled to put on his headset and keyed the radio.

"I just sighted it. Frogfoot. I'm pretty sure it spotted us," he said. "Get ready for it!"

MASSACRE OF THE INNOCENTS

The enemy aircraft popped up over the hills again, this time at the head of the convoy. It dove at a shallow angle towards the ground, a stream of rockets spewing out of the pods slung underneath its wings.

Mohr ducked inside the tank as the blasts ripped through the civilian vehicles. The explosions flung them through the air like cheap plastic toys.

Next came the belch of the aircraft's 30mm main cannon. Thousands of rounds burrowed into the vehicles and the pavement all around. One of them pounded like a fist into the top turret of the Leopard tank.

A series of small fires started. Mohr felt the urge well up within him to bail out but reached for the fire extinguisher instead.

Hoffman shouted in anguished panic.

"Calm down everyone!" Mohr shouted. "Stay focused."

He yanked the pin off the extinguisher while the automatic fire suppression system kicked in. The fog of chemicals filled the tank up and Mohr couldn't see his hand in front of his face for a moment until the venting system did its job.

As the air cleared inside the vehicle, Mohr could see the fires were out. The stench of burnt electronics and wiring filled his nostrils. It was better than being dead - but not by much.

He peered through the PERI system, amazed that the delicate electronics still worked. At the back of the convoy, the Gepard unleashed a torrent of anti-aircraft fire at the Soviet aircraft. The tracers reached up and punched at the Su-25 as it veered slowly to the right. Mohr was sure he could see a couple of holes in the aircraft's fuselage but it was still evidently flyable.

With some measure of relief, he opened the hatch to find Lange still manning the machine gun.

"Lange, get ready! That thing's coming for another pass. I'm sure of it!" he shouted.

The loader aimed his weapon towards the whining sound of the engine after it disappeared behind the hills to the east.

"Heading south again," said Lange. "He's gonna take another pass from the same direction again."

Mohr tried to consider the alternatives to sitting like a painted target but none came to mind. They were completely defenseless.

He tried not to pay any mind to the collection of burnt vehicles all around him. The truck occupants they were helping only seconds later were gone - wiped off the earth, along with the good people who tried to help them. And for what purpose? They were non-combatants. Many of them were children or the elderly.

A dark cloud fell over Mohr. Something inside him broke and snapped off, lost forever to what was happening right here and right now.

The Marders were in ruins, their thin top armor punctured by the hail of cannon rounds. Hauptmann's tank sat there motionless beside the Gepard.

Lange manned the machine gun, ready to fire. Far up ahead, Kessel's tanks tried to pull back under the supposed safety of the Gepard's air defense umbrella. Mohr doubted that they could shoot it down on its third pass. The aircraft already had two holes in it and it seemed to be performing just fine. What difference would two or three more holes make?

"There," said Lange, pointing far up ahead.

The Su-25 pilot popped up his over the hill directly behind the convoy. The plane swooped downward, for another run, its nose pointed straight at the long line of West German vehicles.

The plane thundered along a straight path. Kessel's tanks hammered away at it, the aircraft passing straight in front of the wall of tracers being thrown up at it. The Gepard at the rear of the convoy rushed forward, smashing through the crush of wreckage of civilian cars and trucks to get closer to its target.

It was like watching two gunslingers in the old Western movies. The plane caught a long burst from the Gepard's 35mm auto-cannon and wobbled slightly as it reached the halfway point of the convoy.

The rockets poured out again from under its wings but this time, they landed far to the rear of the mass of vehicles, smashing into the hillside.

The Gepard continued to fire. Its auto cannons whirred, sending 550 rounds per minute up at the incoming plane. Finally, the Su-25 veered away just as the Gepard's auto cannons clicked dry.

The Frogfoot veered left and right like a drunk. The plane traded speed for altitude as it tried to climb over the nearest hill. As it reached the crest, the plane slowed to a hover. Moments before the aircraft pancaked hard against the side of the hill, the canopy broke open and the pilot shot upwards in an ejection seat.

The aircraft's wings snapped off the fuselage as it spun and tumbled down the hill. Its body groaned as it broadsided the tall pines and came to a rest.

With the threat gone, Mohr scanned his surroundings. The road all around him was awash in death. The car in front of him was in flames. Jolted out of a hazy dream, he scrambled out of the tank and called for Lange to bring an extinguisher.

Inside the car, two children sat screaming and crying. The smoke curled up over the insides of the vehicle, obscuring their faces. Mohr felt the intense heat as he stepped forward to smash the nearest window.

The flames licked at him and he took an involuntary step back and coughed. Lange emptied the extinguisher at the base of the fire but it only served to slow the spreading blaze.

The windows on the car began to crack and shatter as the frames melted and sizzled. Mohr reached a hand in past the flames. The fingertips of his fire-resistant gloves melted away.

With a blind grasp, he managed to catch hold of a limp arm. Before he could pull on it, the force of the inferno made him step away. The interior of the car was completely consumed by the conflagration.

Mohr tried a third time to approach the vehicle. Lange dragged him back.

"Sir! No!" he shouted. "We need to get out of here. It's too dangerous."

Mohr tried to shrug off Lange's grip but the big man held him there in place before tearing him back yet again When they reached the rear of the tank, the car exploded.

"Dammit!" shouted Mohr. Tears stung his eyes. "What gives them the right?"

Hoffman emerged from the driver's hatch pointing over to the east.

"Sir, I've got eyes on that Su-25 pilot," he said. "He's up there."

Mohr grabbed his binoculars and aimed them towards the white billowing canopy of the parachute that lay near the top of a steep hill. The pilot lay on the ground, his chute billowing away behind him.

"He's injured. Let's get up there," Mohr said.

The tank pulled away from the road and trudged up the slope. No one said anything as they got closer to where the enemy pilot crawled in the dirt.

"Hoffman, take out the pilot," said Mohr.

The Soviet pilot crawled forward on the dry gravel, his eyes fixed in wide horror at the tank as it thundered straight towards him. As it became clear that the German tank wasn't going to stop after all, he shoved up a hand in the air and howled.

Mohr watched the pilot's expression as the tank kept rolling forwards. For a fraction of an instant, he could have sworn he saw the face of his own father just before the man let out a yelp then disappeared under the treads.

The Leopard traveled a few more meters and then halted. Mohr tried to summon a word to describe the cold unmoving stillness inside of him but there was no way to explain it. His grandfather had never once spoken about the war after it was over. Finally, Mohr understood why.

He checked his watch. By now, Donner and the rest of the battalion would be back at Dingolfing, digging in and preparing for an attack. If Beck was to believed, whatever was left of the 1st Tank Division would cross the bridge to the south and turn straight west to join the attack on Dingolfing.

"Surprised they didn't send their tanks down here for us," said Kessel.

Mohr shrugged. "They have bigger fish to fry. That plane found us by accident. We were a target of opportunity. The main body went right past us to the east. The enemy is bypassing anything smaller than a company and going for the main prize – Landshut."

"I'm insulted."

Mohr watched as his crew poked through the wreckage, looking for any survivors. Their gruesome work was rewarded only once when they found a family of three alive, wandering dazed near the rear of the column. It was nearly dusk by the time their wounds were tended.

The small boy clutched at his mother's chest, screaming over and over. The mother's eyes were glazed over with a faraway look locked inside them.

The father of the child, a man in his early twenties, stood mute. "Are you okay?" Mohr asked the father.

The man responded by pointing to where his car had sat, in between two pickup trucks that were charred and smoldering. The station wagon was crushed in the panic and the family had managed to crawl out through the rear of their vehicle and run away from the carnage.

"Your car?" said Mohr. The man stuttered and mumbled a response, his voice quaking with emotion. He finally gave up trying to speak and simply nodded.

"You need your things?" asked Mohr again. The man simply pointed again and nodded.

"It's okay now. You're safe," he said. Mohr sat him and the rest of the family down on the ground then rushed over to the family's wrecked car, picking through the remains and twisted metal to see what he could find for them.

He managed to dig out some blankets and a few sodas for them then ran over to Hauptmann.

"Any of the Gepard crew make it?" he asked.

Hauptmann shook his head and gestured over to the side of the road where three body bags lay fluttering gently in the breeze. The last of the wounded had hung on for an hour before expiring.

"I saw what you did back there," said Hauptmann. The words came out like a dirge, soft and slow.

"What do you mean?" asked Mohr.

"That pilot. I saw what you did," he repeated, a little louder.

Mohr winced and looked away. "We need to get moving soon," he said. "It's not safe here."

One of Kessel's tanks was heavily damaged from a 30mm round hammering down on the turret, killing the exposed commander and loader instantly.

The remaining ammunition was redistributed among the surviving tanks. Once everything was to Mohr's satisfaction, they said a quick prayer for the sea of dead below them.

He wanted to apologize to each of them for not burying them. There simply wasn't the time or manpower to do it.

When it was finished, Mohr checked that the crews were ready to go, saying quiet words of encouragement to each member. He returned to his tank and raised the battalion commander over the radio. Donner would certainly be wondering where the hell he and his men were by now.

Mohr considered making up an excuse, but he decided then and there that he just didn't care enough anymore. They were fighting the enemy and saving German civilians – just like they were trained to do. Someone who sat in comfortable chair back at HQ hadn't earned the right to question the details, at least not right now anyways.

A look at the reams of paper and the marching orders that Donner had given him showed the planned position of the battalion. At this point, they would be fighting a withdrawal west towards Landshut.

Mohr checked his map. The narrow road he was on took him southwest right between the two cities.

"We could go west towards Route 15 and then go straight south to Landshut. But if we go straight down this road, we may be able to hit their right flank as they come down Route 92," said Mohr. "It's worth a try."

Kessel nodded. "What do we do with the civilians?" he asked. "We can't just leave them here. They have nowhere to go."

Mohr checked the map again. The location of the tiny village of Mengkofen was marked a few kilometers southwest down the road. He pointed to it.

"We drop them off there if the place isn't already wiped off the map."

They got in their tanks. Mohr felt the exhaustion of the day wearing away on him. He was filthy - covered in grease and dirt and blood.

It was hard to believe the war had begun fourteen short hours ago. In that time, he had been through so much along with his men.

The four remaining tanks of Mohr's company continued west along the dark road. Along a curve, they spotted the lights of Mengkofen, a small one-road village surrounded by the first vestige of flat farmland that they had seen all evening.

The four tanks idled while Mohr ordered the gunners to scan the town for any signs of enemy vehicles. The few lone street lamps in the center of town stood like silent glowing sentinels of a way of life that no longer existed. Nothing stirred in the darkness.

"Look. The lights are still on in some of the houses too," said Lange.

Mohr nodded. "They must have left in a big damn hurry."

The tanks rolled through the quiet street and came to a halt. Kessel and Hauptmann took their tanks through the village, checking for any signs of life. A few minutes later, he heard back over the radio from Hauptmann. "I...found something. You better come and look at this."

They drove to the outskirts of the small town to find Hauptmann standing at the side of a large ditch. He stared at Mohr, his expression a mask of undiluted rage. Mohr came over and peered down with a flashlight.

Lined along the bottom of the ditch in neat rows were the bodies of civilians. Entire families had simply been gunned down at the lip and left here to rot. Mohr picked up one of the nearby spent rounds and examined it.

"It's Pact," he said, flinging the brass away in disgust.

"Dogs," spat Hauptmann. "They passed through here and killed everything along the way."

Mohr swore quietly to himself and looked at the young family that sat perched on the tank's hull. He had hoped to find some other people who could help them out. Instead, all they found was an empty shell of a town, its inhabitants slaughtered. Suddenly, the perversity of it all fell into sharp focus.

He knew instantly how things would have to end and why.

Mohr turned to the young sergeant who commanded the Marder and the remaining half-squad of Panzergrenadiers from Muller's platoon.

"We're moving south towards Landshut," he said. "You take the family. Keep them safe. Keep moving west."

The sergeant balked. "What good would that do? We need to get back towards Landshut with you."

Mohr shook his head.

"I have something else in mind," he said. "You need to go now. Someone has to be left after all this is over. Someone has to say what they saw here. What happened. Even what I did back there with that pilot. Someone has to live to say it."

The sergeant nodded but Mohr could see he didn't really understand. That was fine – only obedience mattered. He watched them drive off west, passing through the edge of darkness and disappearing from sight.

Mohr's tanks rolled south along the winding road. He checked his map and listened to the battalion net. It was completely quiet until they reached within three kilometers of Route 92.

Switching to the coded battalion frequency, Mohr picked up the faint panicked transmissions that came from the west. Landshut was falling. The entire battalion was getting pushed back hard.

Lange turned to Mohr. "You really think four tanks can make a difference, sir?"

"No, I don't," he replied. "But it's enough to stand up against what's happening here. Even if it's hopeless. There is a good chance we won't make it. Tell me now if you don't want -."

Lange put a hand up. "Don't say it, sir. Don't you dare say it."

TWILIGHT OF THE GODS

The four Leopard tanks were parked no more than five meters from each other in a copse of trees at the base of a gently sloping hill.

More than a kilometer to the south, past the bumpy uncultivated fields, lay Route 92. The wide strip of highway ran west straight towards Landshut and terminated in Munich.

The jeeps and trucks of the Red Army raced along the road, shuttling vital supplies to feed the Warsaw Pact offensive in southern Germany. These aging and rusted vehicles served as the lifeline that would fuel Communist victory over Western Europe and eventually the world. Taking them out would hurt the enemy very badly and for that reason alone, Mohr was determined to take them out.

He scanned the highway with his thermal sights set to white hot polarity. The outlines of the truck's engines glowed on his little screen as the vehicles laden with ammunition bumbled towards the front.

The scene in front of him was a tank commander's dream. These "soft targets" could easily be destroyed by the high explosive rounds fired by the 105mm main gun. Even the 7.62mm coaxial machine gun could slice through the thin armor.

Why the air forces hadn't swooped in and bombed the hell out of such an obvious target wasn't exactly clear.

Then he saw them.

The camouflage netting made them a little hard to spot at first but Mohr observed patiently until he could discern their shape and identify them.

On the north side of the highway were five tracked vehicles arranged in a circular pattern, each of them about 100 meters apart from the next. They were mobile SA-8 "Osa" launchers, judging from their box-like appearance.

In the middle of them sat the brains of the entire anti-aircraft site. The radar vehicle pointed its curved rectangular dish towards the western sky. It was perched atop a raised berm, giving it a field of view over the trees and low hills to the north of the highway. Several large enemy trucks sat near the site, one of which had a crane for lifting the surface-to-air missiles into the launchers.

Each SA-8 was well-protected from air attack, surrounded by sandbags and hastily-constructed earthworks. They sat silently, waiting for targets to appear. In the night sky above him, the wail of a single-engine jet grew louder.

The radar dish swiveled a few degrees to the right, like a dog sniffing out a rabbit.

A missile on one of the SAM vehicles ignited and leaped up towards its target. Seconds later came a flash in the sky. The jet engine warbled then cut out right before a little ball of flame plummeted to earth. Mohr tracked it visually until it disappeared beyond his field of view to the north.

He turned to Hauptmann, who stood outside of his own Leopard, surveying the highway.

"I'll get the radar and the trucks," he said. "You take the SAMs. Watch your ammo. Kessel stays in reserve in case we need him."

Both men ducked into the turret. Looking through his periscope, Mohr spotted the nearest target and checked the range. "Load SABOT!"

He waited for the loader's response to indicate the armor-piercing ammunition was loaded into the main gun's breach and ready to fire. "Up!" shouted the loader.

Mohr's skin crawled. The old familiar tingle of danger sent a shiver down his body. He was ready. So were his men. He keyed the intercom.

"Gunner, target radar vehicle, 2 o'clock. Range 920. Wait for my signal."

Mohr stood up in his cupola. A second later, Hauptmann also emerged from his tank. They looked at each other and nodded in unison. One. Two. Three.

"Fire!" shouted Mohr.

At the same time, both Leopards rocked backward as their main guns roared. Mohr slipped back down inside the tank and kept his eyes on the monitor.

The radar vehicle erupted into a sphere of brilliant white light as the tank round detonated. The dish spun off the top, hurled like a discus towards the traffic on the nearby highway. A dark gaping hole had been ripped into the side.

Four hundred meters to the left of the destroyed radar vehicle, Hauptmann's main gun round had tunneled into the hull side of an SA-8 launcher. Its missile rack was bent over at a ninety-degree angle, pointing straight down at the ground.

Hauptmann's turret rotated to the left slightly, finding the next hapless target.

One of the SAM site's supply trucks drove up the hill towards the highway. "Load HEAT," Mohr said calmly. Beside him, Lange slid the round into the breach and slammed it forward.

"Up!" he shouted.

This was the most dangerous time. If Mohr showed too much excitement, his men would forget their training and make mistakes. He took a deep breath, telling himself to calm down. He spoke the words slowly into his intercom.

"Gunner. Target. Truck. 12 o'clock. Wait for it!"

The truck ambled up onto the highway, jammed full of supply trucks and light vehicles. It nearly tipped over as it joined the pan-icked procession.

"Fire!" shouted Mohr!

"On the way!" came the reply.

The truck exploded as the round impacted, the missiles inside detonating along with it. A flash of light engulfed several vehicles on the highway and a wave of boiling red flame swept along the length of the road.

"Dear God!" mouthed Mohr. The destruction rippled outward, igniting the column of vehicles and spreading like a hungry demon. Everything in its path was consumed by the conflagration.

Chaos and confusion erupted around the SAM site. It was teeming with men who were scrambling out of their vehicles in a desperate bid to get away from the growing wildfire.

"Gunner! Get the coax on that SAM site!" he shouted.

The machine gun spat out the rounds at a rate of a thousand per minute. The exposed crewmen and infantry near the site scrambled for cover or fell where they stood. The rest of Mohr's tanks fired at the remaining vehicles and men until finally, the last SAM vehicle was a pile of burning scrap.

As Lange and Vogel hosed down the target area with automatic weapons fire, Mohr heard Hauptmann's tank reverse from its position. He turned to see the sergeant's tank stop and fire a high explosive round into the jumble of wreckage and vehicles near the highway.

Mohr commanded his own driver to start moving and the four tanks began leapfrogging backward over the hill to their rear.

Just as his tank neared the crest, Mohr heard a deep belching sound from far ahead. He looked up to see a pair of cross-shaped A-10 Warthogs dive towards the highway, smoke bursting from the nose of each plane where the 30mm cannon was located.

The cannon's shells, each taller than a long-necked bottle of beer, drilled easily down through the top of the supply trucks and lightly armored vehicles on the pavement.

They leveled out at no more than a couple hundred feet above the highway and followed it for a few seconds before dropping the cluster munitions from their wings. All the way back to the highway junction near the city, the road lit up like a huge torch, engulfing the mass of hapless men and machines.

A sudden panicked thought came over Mohr. "They don't know we're friendly," he said to himself. "They might come for us next!"

Mohr watched in horror as the A-10s suddenly peeled off their attack run and turned towards them. With each passing second, they grew larger.

Mohr ducked down inside his tank. "Move!" he shouted. "Driver! Zigzag backward as fast as you can go!"

The massive tank shifted direction as it reversed over the crest and slalomed downhill. Ten seconds later came the series of thuds and bangs around the tank as the aircraft rounds landed. Mohr's ears rang and sparks flew from the electrical components around his cupola.

The jets roared past Mohr's position and turned back west. Relieved, Mohr commanded his tanks to continue heading south towards the highway.

"Let's keep this going," he said. "Move along the road. Hit as much as you can and don't let up. Stop for nothing."

The four tanks took an echelon left formation and drove beside the wreckage of the highway. Vogel brought the main gun over, firing at the dazed survivors of the bombing run. Lange added to the destruction with his own machine gun.

Nothing fired back.

Nothing survived.

Everything alive was merely cut down as the tanks drove together, shooting at anything that moved. The remainder burned.

Five hundred meters on, they found the first enemy vehicles that had not been obliterated by the A-10 pass. Before the enemy could react, Mohr's tanks destroyed them.

Just ahead, Mohr spotted several jeeps and trucks surrounding large canvas tents that sat concealed just off the main road. Several of the vehicles had long antennas attached securely to their roof.

"I've got a command post of some sort," said Mohr. "Let's take it out."

As the nearby enemy tanks burned, the infantry scattered across the road and into prepared positions. An RPG round slammed squarely into Mohr's front turret, the Leopard shuddered to a halt. Automatic fire slapped at the outside of the tank as Hoffman tried to get the tank moving again.

Behind them, the other three tanks poured fire at the command post. The HEAT rounds slammed into the tents and the thin-skinned vehicles. At last, Mohr's tank reversed away from the danger.

Hauptmann swung his tank over to the left and shot at the infantry on the flank. Bodies of soldiers lay everywhere while their comrades scattered into the night.

Mohr ordered his tanks to keep going along the highway, pushing on towards the west. He wondered how long it would take before the Czechs realized what was happening and react to it. The tanks rolled along the pavement in pairs, driving among the oblivious supply trucks and troop trucks.

The nearest jeep was ripped apart by a high explosive round. The other drivers veered off the highway, several of the larger trucks overturning in the scramble to get away from the nearby enemy tanks. Mohr's tanks were wolves running amidst the sheep. The prey was theirs to take at will.

As they sped down the road west towards Landshut, Mohr spotted the cooling tower of the Isar nuclear reactor. Crowded around it were dozens of artillery pieces and what looked like several tanks. He shook his head as they approached.

Of course, the enemy would mass reserve troops and howitzers near a nuclear reactor - no one would dare hit it from the air.

"Okay, we go for everything around the reactor," he said over the radio. "Hit everything you can around there."

The artillery guns near the reactor fired off their shells to the west. Mohr pulled off south of the main road with the other tanks and began shooting. Unlike the attack on the command post minutes earlier, the enemy seemed prepared for them.

The first sign of their forewarning came when Kessel's tank was struck by an anti-tank missile. A dozen meters to Mohr's left, the vehicle simply burst apart, a brief and brilliant flash in the night.

Mohr spoke to Vogel. "Target the artillery guns."

Hauptmann's tank drove west along the highway, hitting the enemy parked around the perimeter of the main buildings and the cooling tower.

Several of the T-72s shot back in Mohr's direction. Hoffman reversed, trying to find a spot where the hull wasn't exposed to the incoming rounds. Vogel fired the main gun at the field guns. The targets were grouped together so closely that one round was often enough to destroy two of them at the same time.

Something slammed into the tank. The lights inside the vehicle died. Mohr's monitor faded to a blank screen. He looked into the inky blackness of the PERI optics and shook his head.

"I've lost my range-finder!" shouted Vogel. "Switching to manual."

"Keep firing," said Mohr. "Just keep shooting."

Mohr threw open the hatch and watched as Hauptmann's tank was destroyed by a pair of T-72 rounds. The first shot dug through the hull side, leaving a glowing half circle to mark where the armor was pierced.

The second round struck a few seconds later, carving into the side of the turret where the penetrator had burrowed. No one got out of the tank.

Several T-72s came screaming down the highway, their main guns firing in near-unison. The only remaining tank under Mohr's command was destroyed as it fired back at the oncoming enemies.

Hoffman drove over the hump of the road while Vogel kept firing into the mass of troops, vehicles, and artillery around the nearby reactor. The first T-72 round hit Mohr's Leopard somewhere around the armored skirts near the treads. The tank stopped and Mohr released the smoke grenades, hoping they would give his men just enough cover to abandon the tank.

"Everyone out," he declared.

Lange climbed down from the hatch while an enemy round whizzed over the Leopard. He slid down the tank while Hoffman scrambled out and ran for the cover of the nearby woods. Vogel fired again, refusing to leave the stricken vehicle. The man's choice had been made.

Mohr left him.

He slid over the turret as the machine gun rounds sliced through the air all around him.

Something struck him in the shoulder hard and he tumbled to the ground.

Surrounded by darkness and smoke, the world was reduced to a series of deafening impressions that flashed across his conscious mind. He had to get out of here.

Mohr slowly reached out to lift himself up with his good shoulder. Something shoved him back. A lightning bolt of pain cut across his chest. Everything went dark.

EPILOGUE

The Leopard sat on the side of the road at dawn the next morning. The remnants of the 24th Panzer Battalion drove east down the road, past the twisted wreckage of two Czechoslovakian divisions.

Colonel Donner jumped out of his Wolf jeep to witness the destruction in and around the highway. The nuclear reactor, still intact, was awash with the detritus of the previous night's battle.

Four West German tanks were among the countless enemy dead and wounded strung for miles along the road.

The bodies of the West German tank crews were placed carefully alongside the road. Donner bent down to find the face of Kurt Mohr staring back up at him. How could he ever repay this debt?

The colonel kneeled and said a quick silent prayer. As it came to a close, a broken groan spilled out from Mohr. Donner stood up and waved his arms toward the traffic that swept by on the road.

"Medic!" he shouted. "We need a medic over here!"

EXPECTED SOVIET ADVANCE
FIGHTIN POSITIONS MULLER
FIGHTIN POSITIONS TANKS
OBERHIRSCHBERG
DATTING
Route 11
DISSENBACH
DEPLOYMENT POSITIONS
GRAFLING
EIDSBERG

LEGACY OF A LEOPARD: A LOOK BACK
by Gen. Edgar Wynne, US Army (ret'd.)

The following article is an excerpt from Line of Fire Monthly published in 1989:

By 1985, the Leopard 1 series of main battle tanks was a dinosaur. Despite its widespread adoption among Western armies, the twenty-year old main battle tank was a full generation behind the armored vehicles that were coming online by the war's beginning.

Crews that fought in the Leopard 1 were forced to use the vehicle's speed and agility to gain an advantage on the battlefield. Many tankers who failed to use its greatest assets in battle would learn of the weaknesses too late when a Soviet shell crashed through their armor.

While the M1 Abrams and Leopard 2 were coated with armor created with advanced technologies, the older Leopard 1 hull and turret consisted of sloped rolled homogenous steel. By the mid-80s, this level of protection was wholly inadequate for surviving a hit from the newer Soviet tanks, most notably the T-72 and the T-80.

After the war's end, studies of action reports revealed that Leopard 1 loss rates when engaged with frontline Soviet tanks were appalling. A direct hit on the front armor from a T-72 had a nearly 90 percent success rate for knocking out the vehicle at distances of up to three kilometers. Similar results were reported against the T-62, which fired rounds that could penetrate the Leopard 1 up to 1800 meters away.

Enemy tanks were not the only problem Leopard commanders faced on the battlefield. Nearly 36 percent of total vehicle losses were blamed on wire-guided anti-tank missiles, which almost always required a stationary target in order to achieve a hit.

Infantry armed with rocket-propelled grenades accounted for over 10 percent of Leopard 1 losses throughout the war. Any time the enemy was allowed to get behind the vehicle and manage a rear shot to the hull, the result was almost always a kill.

Summarily, the Leopard 1 was extraordinarily vulnerable when it stayed in one place and got bogged down in battle. Commanders learned very quickly to keep the tank moving and in cover or face almost certain death from any number of weapons systems. On a mechanized and highly mobile battlefield, the training and skill required to merely stay alive seems almost superhuman.

In terms of offense, the tank proved to be a deadly adversary in the right hands. Those who understood its limitations and employed its strengths were able to make the Leopard 1 punch far above its weight class. In Central Europe, the tank scored an 85 percent hit rate while on the move. This number rose to 92 percent when firing from a stationary position.

Before the war began, critics of the Leopard 1 complained that the tank's 105mm gun would fail to penetrate the front armor of newer Soviet MBTs like the T-72 and T-80. Post-war studies have since shown that this was not the case. In fact, when firing on such targets at similar ranges, there appears to be almost no difference in enemy kill rate when compared with the Leopard 2's 120mm gun.

The major contrast between the performance of the two weapons systems seems to be the range at which these kills were achieved. On the flat land of the Central European Plain, the Leopard 2 was able to engage targets further out and thereby inflict significantly greater enemy losses.

In Southern Germany, where the rugged and hilly terrain meant closer engagement ranges, the gap between the 120mm and 105mm kill rates virtually disappeared. By all accounts, the Leopard 1 was just as deadly as a third generation tank in situations that played to its strengths.

Most interviews with Leopard 1 tank commanders attribute the tank's success to continual upgrades of the fire control system. A second factor was the enhanced crew training and tactics that were taught to company commanders in the years just prior to the conflict.

By 1985, no less than five versions of Leopard 1s had been produced since the first one entered service in 1965. The most recent incarnation by then was the Leopard 1A4, which boasted a number of important features that proved critical for success in a combat environment.

The most important of these was the PERI R12 system, which gave the commander an independent sight from the gunner. A small monitor was added in the commander's station that could be operated in thermal or day mode. This offered the commander a view of the battlefield from within the protected confines of the turret. Needless to say, the PERI greatly enhanced coordination between the gunner and tank commander.

The benefits of this increased situational awareness extended to platoon leaders and company commanders. In this way, the technology worked as a combat multiplier rather than just another "fancy gadget", as some critics had decried the PERI prior to the war.

Another major factor that led to the Leopard's success in combat was the revolution in military affairs that took place during the late 1970s and early 1980s in the West. As the Soviet investment in military equipment and training ballooned during these years, the West Germans adapted to the growing threat by addressing perceived shortcomings in their operational and tactical doctrine and structure.

The most notable of these changes took place in 1982 with the implementation of Heeresstruktur 4 (Army Structure 4) by the Bundeswehr. The plan called for a renewed emphasis on combat reconnaissance and tactics aimed at addressing the newly-emerging military technology that the Soviet Union and its allies were deploying at an alarming rate.

In May 1985, West German tank commanders would employ the full extent of this training to seize the initiative from their numerically superior foe again and again.

Little did the architects of Army Structure 4 realize that they were not only setting new standards for the West German military, but they were also dictating how the war would be conducted on German soil.

At the company level, effective use of the Leopard 1 tank was a matter of putting this training into good use not only to achieve mission objectives but for the very survival of the vehicle and its crew.

ABOUT THE AUTHOR

Brad Smith is a freelance writer and game designer. He has a keen interest in the topic of the late Cold War, which has fed his creative output. He has authored around a dozen books set in an alternate World War III: 1985 universe. His blog can be found at: www.hexsides.com. You can also access his books on the Amazon.com store page. Several of his stories are available through Lock 'n Load Publishing.

His main interests are writing, wargaming, and spending time with his wife and son. He recently designed "NATO Air Commander" and the soon to be released "That Others May Live" both published by Hollandspiele. Two of his favorite wargames are "Gulf Strike" and "The Korean War" from Victory Games. His gaming blog can be found at: www.hexsides.blogspot.com.

Brad has worked as an Emergency Medical Responder in Canada then as a writer based in Geneva, Switzerland before moving to Japan in 2004, where he has lived ever since. He holds a Bachelor's degree majoring in History from the University of Winnipeg, a Master's in Journalism from the University of British Columbia, and a dual Master's degree in TESOL and Applied Linguistics from the University of Leicester. He has written for academic journals, newspapers, radio, and magazines on a variety of topics. He recently served as an editor for an issue of Yaah! magazine and is a frequent contributor to other game journals.

His main writing inspirations include Tom Clancy, Joe Scalzi, Ralph Peters, and Stephen King. His favorite books include "Red Storm Rising", "Old Man's War", and "Red Army".

ABOUT THE EDITOR
- Hans Korting -

I have been reading books about (military) aviation history all of my life, and this way the connection with military history is easily made. Main interest is WWII, but I also enjoy reading up on and playing games about WWI, modern-era warfare, the American Civil War, Napoleonics, and more. First game ever was bought in an American book store in Amsterdam, Avalon Hill's D-Day '77. Next game was SPI's Arnhem, and a whole range of games has followed since. Putting my hands, or rather eyes, where my mouth is, I next decided to help out proofreading rulebooks. Some gaming magazines were next, like War Diary magazine. I also write about boardwargames for Ducosim's (DutchConflictSimulation) Spel! magazine, and sometimes try to write a decent article for a magazine too. Daytime job is at a small insurance broker as a claims handler.

AUDIO BOOK EDITION
- Narrated By: Keith Tracton -

Keith Tracton has been acting in some way, shape, or form for thirty-seven years. A veteran of stage, screen, TV, film, voiceovers and, of course, audiobook narration. His audiobooks can be found on iTunes and on Audible.com. The only thing he has been doing longer than acting is playing board war games - forty-four years doing that, and still going strong. As such, he also very much considers himself fortunate to be the lead developer for Lock 'n Load Publishing's upcoming alternate-WWIII platoon level game series **World At War 85**.

WHAT IS WORLD AT WAR 85 GAME SERIES
- by David Heath -

I am the Director of Operations at Lock 'n Load Publishing, where we produce both tabletop and computer games with a strategy theme. So what made us publish a book of short stories? The love of gaming. These short stories were inspired by the kind of stories friends share about games they played and the adventures they experienced while playing them. Those stories always remind me of the kind told by my Dad, his friends, and my own buddies who spent time in the service.

The idea for this book series started from a long desire to hear the stories of other gamers, and to share my love for gaming. This project became real thanks to Brad Smith, Hans Korting, Keith Tracton, and many others. Without their support this never would have happened. While talking this over it became clear we weren't the only ones who enjoyed telling and listening to gaming adventures.

This story use a number of things from our World at War 85 game series, specifically the names units and even the occasional moments inspired by game events. This added a new level to our stories and added the ability and similarity for these men to live on in each of our games.

Some of you may be wondering what the World at War 85 game series is all about. The World at War 85 (WaW85) series is a dynamic platoon-level tactical combat board game series centered on armored combat from the 1980s in a fictional World War III setting. With unparalleled artwork and a formation based game mechanic that keeps both players constantly involved, each action-packed engagement plays out cinematically. Decisions need to be made quickly. Tactical leadership is key. Unique abilities and synergies enhance effectiveness. And detailed objectives based ont he scenario layout encourages bold gameplay. There is even a Solo module for those quiet nights at home.

Platoon combat is central to WaW85, but besides Heavy Armor and Soft Armor units, we have Support Weapon such as mortars, heavy machine guns, and anti-tank guns. There are also Helicopters, faction Leaders, fixed-wing Close Air Support and an in depth suit of Artillery options, both on and off-board. Individuals such as Leaders, Special Weapons Teams, and, of course, Special Forces, complete the forces available for each side. We also have free downloadable game walkthroughs, making the game series more accessible to new players more than ever.

Whether you are a fan of 80s-era military fiction or the World War 3 setting, the WaW85 series has you covered with a variety of boxed games and expansions, including an evolving storyline to follow as you play through ear game in the series. With WaW85 the gaming never ends. It's Platoon-level tactical combat at its best!

WORLD AT WAR 85 NOVELS

SOMETHING THE SOVIETS DIDN'T PLAN ON

It is May 1985 and World War III rages in Central Europe. Fledgling insurgent groups in the East Bloc fight for independence from their Soviet overlords. America pledges to help. Among the teams of US military advisers are two Vietnam War veterans, sent in to assist an East German major named Werner Brandt and his motley band of fighters. Their objectives are to help destroy Soviet military reinforcements as they speed towards the frontlines and to eliminate the Russian garrison in control of Saxony. It won't be easy – Brandt is consumed with a lust for vengeance that threatens to derail his own operations.

Captain Joe Ricci and Sergeant Ned Littlejohn are about to enter a combat zone for the first time in nearly fifteen years. With them, they bring the scarred memories of their Vietnam experiences. As the stakes climb higher and the battle to survive grows more intense, each decision could lead to the liberation of a nation or their own downfall.

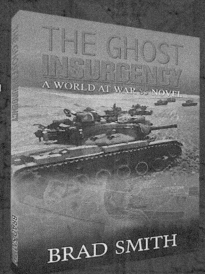

THE SOVIET INVASION CONTINUES

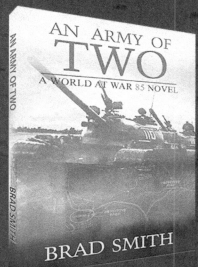

First Lieutenant Darren White is trapped behind enemy lines with the remnants of his cavalry troop. Together with his second-in-command, Maurice Fitzgerald, he waits for the right opportunity to strike back at the Russians in occupied West Germany.

As they conduct joint operations with a Special Forces team in the Fulda Gap, a terrible secret is uncovered. The Soviets have found a sure-fire way to win the war. It's up to White and Fitzgerald to stop them. A daring operation might just be enough to make or break the Soviet war effort in Fulda. Will Fitzgerald and White's personal differences doom the attempt?

LOCK 'N LOAD PUBLISHING
WWW.LNLPUBLISHING.COM

STORMING THE GAP
WORLD AT WAR 85

World War III has Begun

STORMING THE GAP is the first volume in the new WORLD AT WAR 85 SERIES, a line of games centered on fast and furious platoon-level combat. Set in an alternate history 1985, the globe is thrust into the maelstrom of World War III when the Warsaw Pact armies storm across the border between East and West Germany in a gamble to seize West Germany, and the whole of Free Europe.

Fight the opening battles of World War III; from desperate delaying actions by US Armored Cavalry and West German Panzergrenadier forces to determined counterattacks by local ad-hoc armored forces against the might of the Soviet hordes. Strike fast with Soviet Air Assault troops in heliborne ops, securing roadways to allow the massed armor columns of the PACT to sweep westward into Germany. The devastating armed forces of West Germany, the United States, East Germany, and the Soviet Union are at your disposal in your quest to reshape the world and history.

The weight of the tactical decisions rests solely on your shoulders. Can NATO slow the Soviet advance with the armor and infantry they can bring to bear? Or skillfully use Close Air Support and Attack Helicopter units to swing the tide of battle in your favor? Can the PACT slice through into Germany and cross the Rhine river, gateway to the conquest of all of Europe?

LOCK 'N LOAD
PUBLISHING
WWW.LNLPUBLISHING.COM

CPSIA information can be obtained
at www.ICGtesting.com
Printed in the USA
LVHW052242251119
638495LV00003B/460/P

9 781733 104111